James Clark Strong

Wah-kee-nah and Her People

The Curious Customs, Traditions, and Legends of the North American Indians

James Clark Strong

Wah-kee-nah and Her People
The Curious Customs, Traditions, and Legends of the North American Indians

ISBN/EAN: 9783337062026

Printed in Europe, USA, Canada, Australia, Japan

Cover: Foto ©ninafisch / pixelio.de

More available books at **www.hansebooks.com**

WAH-KEE-NAH.

WAH-KEE-NAH

AND HER PEOPLE

THE CURIOUS CUSTOMS, TRADITIONS, AND LEGENDS OF THE NORTH AMERICAN INDIANS

BY

JAMES C. STRONG

BVT. BRIG.-GEN. VETERAN RESERVE CORPS, U.S.A.

G. P. PUTNAM'S SONS

NEW YORK   LONDON
27 WEST TWENTY-THIRD STREET   24 BEDFORD STREET, STRAND

The Knickerbocker Press

1893

Electrotyped, Printed and Bound by
The Knickerbocker Press, New York
G. P. PUTNAM'S SONS

PREFACE.

WHEN the white man first came to make his home in the New World, that portion of it which now constitutes the United States and its Territories was inhabited by probably upwards of a million Indians, who, so far as we know, were the aborigines of the country. Their numbers are now reduced to about two hundred and fifty thousand, and none of these can be properly called "Wild Indians," as all of them are now gathered upon reservations, under the charge of agents of the United States, and supplied at certain periods, with food and clothing furnished by the Government. Those in British Columbia are also gathered upon reservations and cared for by the Canadian Government.

I began to live among the Indians upon the Pacific Coast in 1850, learned one of their languages, and for six years travelled with and among them.

Like most others who have lived with them and become familiar with their folk-lore, habits, and home life, my sympathies became strongly enlisted in their behalf. The exceptions to this state of feeling I have found chiefly among those who, living with or near them, have coveted their land, and as a rule scrupled at nothing as a means of obtaining it ; and, to ease their conscience, or justify their conduct, have decried and vilified the Indian as a monster in human shape which they were justified in exterminating.

It does not seem to me that these are as competent to testify to the true character of the Indian as those who have lived among them as friends, with no motive other than that of studying this remarkable but unfortunate primitive race.

This book was begun at the solicitation of friends, who desired me to put in writing my experience among the "Wild Indians" of forty years ago, together with the traditions and legends related to me by their aged men and women, whose memories ran back to a time when no white man had made his appearance upon the Pacific Coast, except in Alaska.

In doing this, and as I recalled my life among the Indians and remembered that wherever I had found them in their primitive state they were kind and hospitable, always more ready to do a favor than an injury, the question forced itself upon me, Why is it that after a short association with the whites, these people became changed in character? and this question has led to a review of the treatment received by them at the hands of the white men. In this I have endeavored to look upon the events narrated, from the Indian's point of view—through *his eyes,* as it were,—and thus to appreciate more clearly the natural effect which such events would be likely to have upon the feelings and actions of any other man in his place.

I have written of these people as I have found them in my life among them; have related my personal experience with them; and have treated of their habits, customs, traditions, and legends as I have seen and heard them.

Although not originally written for publication, I have concluded to place these pages before my countrymen and countrywomen, hoping that they may not only entertain the reader, but also serve to lessen the blame attached to the Indian for the acts of retaliation (often savage and brutal, it must be admitted) which the white man's treatment of him has incited; and with the further hope of inducing those who read, to *think* upon one of the great questions of the day—how to solve the Indian problem.

Much that is herein written has been gathered from original sources and personal experience; but for the brief outlines of Indian history from the time that these people first became known to the white man down to the year 1850, I am indebted to the historians of the American continent—an indebtedness which I take pleasure in thus generally acknowledging.

I have called this book "Wah-kee-nah and Her People," in grateful memory of a beautiful Indian maiden who saved my life at imminent risk of her own, and whose story forms a brief episode herein.

J. C. S.

BUFFALO, N. Y.

CONTENTS.

CHAPTER I.

PAGE

Introduction—Character of primitive Indians—Interesting incidents—Massacre of the Pequots—King Philip's war. . . . 1

CHAPTER II.

Incidents continued—Effect upon the Indians—Sources of trouble—Capt. John Smith and Pocahontas—Marriage and death of the Indian princess—Indian chief killed for taking a tin can to make a tobacco-box—The Ho-de-no-sau-nee, Iroquois, or Six Nations—Their "totems"—Wampum belts, how made; their use—Progress in agriculture—Councils—The calumet and its use—Councils for the women—Marriage—Indian's argument in favor of easy divorce. 13

CHAPTER III.

Dances—Ancient war dance—Liberating a live bird as a part of the burial ceremony—Religious belief—A chief's reason for not embracing the white man's religion—Totem or record post—Game of ball with the Eries—Foot-race—Wrestling for life—The vanquished tomahawked by his infuriated chief—Battle between the Eries and the Iroquois—Sa-go-ye-wat-ta—His speech—Tah-gah-jute—His love for the whites—His family butchered—His revenge—His speech. 29

CHAPTER IV.

PAGE

Superstitions—Soi-en-ga-rah-ta's dream—How he was out-witted—Joseph Brant, the Mohawk chieftain—How he saved the lives of the white women and children after the battle of Springfield—Indian's dress—How it was made before the whites came—How ornamented — Children — Pappoose board, how carried and how disposed of—Indians west of the Iroquois—Their habits—Simon Kenton—How he stole the Indians' horses —How he was captured—Running the gauntlet—His escape—Western tribes—Their religious belief—Their war dance—Other dances. 46

CHAPTER V.

The Sioux, or Dakotas—Their strength—Weapons—Singular cap—Their reasons for taking scalps—Their reason for not tak-ing them—Their belief in regard to the appearance of persons in the spirit land—Curious manner of insulting the enemy—Lan-guage of feathers—How they dispose of their dead—The red hand—How the young men wooed their brides—Stealing a bride —Marriage ceremony in high life—Superstitions in regard to the ceremony—Superstitions relating to idiots and insane persons—How Prof. Hayden was benefited by this—Doctors, or medicine men—How made—How called for—The sacred rattle—How made—How the medicine men heal the sick—The spirit of an animal in the body—How drawn out and forced into a piece of bark—How the spirit is shot and burned—The doctor's troubles. 62

CHAPTER VI.

Story of Wi-jun-jon—How he kept count of the white men's houses on his journey to Washington—His disgust—His meta-morphose—The superstition in regard to him on his return to his own country—Had learned to lie like white men—How the evil spirit in him was overcome with the bale of an old iron pot—Stoicism—How children are taught to be stoics—Battle with the hornets—Oratory of the chief "Two Stars"—The Mandans—

Their belief that the eyes in a portrait moved—Their curious
ideas relating to it—Buffalo hunting—The usual manner of
catching and taming the wild horse—The Comanches—Their
mode of breaking in wild horses.   79

CHAPTER VII.

The northern Indians—How they built their houses—Windows
made of ice—How they caught deer—The " kaiak"—Their
fires—How made—Their unique manner of killing the polar
bear — Marriage — The Koniagas — Their ornaments — The
" parka," how made—The Aleuts—Their weapons and domestic
implements—How they caught the bear—Games—The Thlinkeets—Peculiar hat—Slaves—Stone pipes—Marriage ceremony
lasting four weeks.   93

CHAPTER VIII.

The Tinneh family—Superstitions in regard to dancing—Superstition in regard to cutting the finger nails of a female child—
Hiaquas as money—Efficacy of a chief's teepee, and his clothes—
When the doctors must return the fee—Slavery—Widow compelled to mount the funeral pyre of her husband, as in India—
When allowed to escape burning to death—How the husband's
ashes are disposed of for two years—Pottery, how made—Binding
the feet of female infants, as in China—Their reasons for going to
war—The Haidahs—How labor is divided—Salt—Hunting the
whale—Complexion—Houses high in the air—Singular harpoons—How they make their bows—Pipes carved from stone—
Immense canoes, how made—Musical instruments—Blankets,
how woven—Peculiar breed of dogs that they sheared like
sheep—Superstitions in regard to marriage—Ceremony on the
water—How they gambled—The Nootkas—Short hair—Flattening the head—Adornment of the women—When they considered
themselves old, and ceased such adornment—Amusements—Love
powder and its uses—Puget Sound Indians—How they caught
wild fowl.   106

CHAPTER IX.

PAGE

The Chinooks—"Aunt Sally"—Exciting occurrence while fastening a whale—Salmon, how caught—Expedition to the Cascades for slaves—Attempted suicide of a chief's daughter, rather than become a slave—What she found on arriving at her captor's home—Buying freedom—Story of two slave boys who were to be killed to wait upon their master in the spirit land—Burial of their master—Little slave boy tied to the death post—How rescued—"Must I eat all this?"—The belief of the Chinooks in spirits—Legend in regard to mountains—Legend of the Cascades—Submerged forests—Mount St. Helen's "got angry."   .   . 122

CHAPTER X.

Indians' fidelity to friends—Wah-kee-nah—Her costume—Shooting her first deer—How she saved the life of my brother's little boy—Her perilous adventure with mountain wolves—Attacked by a panther—Her escape—How she saved my life at the risk of her own—Her lover Le-lim—His persistency rewarded—Wah-kee-nah the bride of the chieftain's son.   .   .   .   137

CHAPTER XI.

Yakima war—Quotations from Maj. Genl. Wool's report of that war—Bravery of a white woman and her daughter—How the husband and father was killed—Their house set on fire with fire arrows—How the women killed four Indians—The mother struck with an arrow—Their miraculous escape—A little Indian boy killed by a white man for trying to defend his mother—Story of an Indian who was shot by a white man because he would not trade horses.   157

CHAPTER XII.

Marriage ceremony among the river Chinooks—How it differed from that in the mountainous country—Exciting race on horseback for a bride—Four suitors in the race—The one who

PAGE

first caught her to have her—Her wedding ceremony—Evil omens
—How propitiated—Wedding presents—No credit in connubial
matters—How Indians hide their tracks—How they leave signs
for friends to follow—An elk hunt—How I found the guides—
Gambling—Indian's offer to wager his wife against my canoe
upon a game with beaver's teeth—How I won the beaver's teeth—
Why Indians gamble.   167

CHAPTER XIII.

Incident relating to the Indians south of the thirty-third parallel
of north latitude—Indians apt scholars in the art of treachery—
How taught them—Identity of woman's mind—Wanton cruelty
toward the Indians—Woman chief—Her necklace of pearls—
What became of it—She taken prisoner and held as a hostage by
the whites—Her escape—Burning Indians at the stake by the
whites to make them tell where the gold mines were—Cutting
both hands off all the chiefs.   183

CHAPTER XIV.

The Miccosukies—William Bartram—Scenes at a great chief's
death-bed—Dr. Henry Perrine—Hiding his family under a
wharf—Their experience when the wharf took fire—Dr. Perrine's
death—Miraculous escape of the family—Laws of the Seminoles
as to marriage—Death for marrying a white person—Singular
custom of the Pawnees—How they cut their hair before the introduction of knives or shears—Growing the scalp lock—Beauty
of their wild horses—Pawnee agriculture—Flattening the head
among the Chocktaws and Chickasaws—The Comanches—Reports in regard to their primitive character—Reports of their
present character.   194

CHAPTER XV.

Anahuac, or Maheco — Arrival of Cortes — An unnatural
mother—A cazique's daughter made a slave—Rescued by accident—Becomes an interpreter—Indian General Tuetile—Indian

PAGE

Governor Pilpato—Singular salutation—Description of the
presents brought by the Indian general—His speech on present-
ing them—How the whites displayed their power—Indian artists
—Indian system of chirography—Gold a cure for disease of the
heart—More presents—Description of them—Indian general's
speech—Reply—The Indian's anger—Cazique of Cempoala—
How to make brave soldiers—Destruction of the Cempoalan's
idols—The wonderful legend in regard to Quetzalcoatl—The
belief that he or his descendants would return—His return feared
by the rulers—Battle between the whites and the Tlascalans—
Indian belief that the whites derived their power from the sun—
Battle in the night—Cutting off the hands of the Indians by the
whites.   209

CHAPTER XVI.

Peace made with the Tlascalans—Speech of the Tlascalan
general—Reply—More presents from the Indian emperor—Description of them—Fine agriculture—Stone arched bridge—
Description of the Indian reception at Tlascala—Evergreen
arches, festoons, etc.—Description of the city—Four hundred
Indian maidens given to the white soldiers—Indian advice showing true friendship—Six thousand Tlascalan soldiers join the
whites—Description of the country between Tlascala and Cholula—The entry into the city of Cholula—Description of the
Cholulans—Conspiracy to destroy the Spaniards—Their guardian
angel—Conspiracy discovered—The slaughter of five thousand
Indians—The emperor's fear—Extract from the speech made
at his accession to the throne—Description of more of his
presents—Agriculture and horticulture in the valley—Description
of the valley—The emperor's resolve not to oppose the whites
—More presents, and a large bribe. 226

CHAPTER XVII.

Town over the water—Stone houses—Indians shot down—
Cazique of Texcuco—His palanquin—Presentation of pearls—
Causeways—Floating gardens—Iztapalapan—Its architecture—

PAGE

Beautiful gardens—Garden reservoir and fountain—Cortes met
by several hundred Indian chiefs—Drawbridge—Approach of
the emperor—His palanquin—Description of the ceremony on
meeting—Description of the emperor—The entry into the
capital—Description of the Indians in the city—Visit of the
emperor—Description of the gifts he brought—Firing the artillery—Dismay of the Indians—Visit to the emperor—Manner of
approaching him—The emperor's reply to the speech of the
whites—Description of the palace—Description of the city—
Dishes, how made—Dresses of the women.   242

CHAPTER XVIII.

Division of the presents among the whites—Their value in
dollars, and pounds sterling—Arrest of the emperor—The burning alive of a cazique, his son, and fifteen chiefs, by the Spaniards—Butchery of several hundred Indians while attending a
festival—Death of the emperor while a prisoner—The whites
driven from the city—They recapture the city, by the aid of
caziques who still believe the whites to be descendants of the
" God of the Air "—Guatemozin, the ruler after the death of the
emperor—Tortured and hanged after being promised protection—Sacrifice of human beings by the whites—Indian records
and books burned—Growth of civilization among the Indians—
What the United States and Canada are doing for the Indians—
Broken promises the cause of Indian wars—Why they should be
made citizens—How now situated—Indian judges and juries—
Assistant farmers—How one of them planted turnips—Schools
for Indian children—Indian agents—White crows—Motive for
becoming an Indian agent—Reasons for putting the Indians
under the care of the War Department—Agricultural schools—
Conclusion.   258

WAH-KEE-NAH AND HER PEOPLE.

CHAPTER I.

THE researches and discoveries of the anthropologist prove conclusively that North America has been inhabited by human beings for countless ages. It is, however, outside of my purpose, and of the scope of this volume, to enter into any discussion of the facts upon which that conclusion is based.

"Originally, for a savage wilderness, there was here a dense population. Before the advent of Europeans, America counted its aborigines by millions; among whom might be found every phase of primitive humanity, from the reptile-eating cave-dweller of the Great Basin, to the Aztec and Maya-Guiche civilization of the table-land;—a civilization characterized by Dr. Draper as one 'that might have instructed Europe, a culture wantonly crushed by Spain, who therein destroyed races more civilized than herself.'"

Mr. Bancroft says: "In the study of mankind, everything connected therewith becomes of import-

ance. There is not a feature of primitive humanity
without significance, nor a custom or characteristic
of savage nations, however mean or revolting to us,
from which important lessons may not be drawn. It
is only from the study of barbarous and partially
cultivated nations that we are able to comprehend
man as a progressive being, and to recognize the
successive stages through which our savage ancestors
have passed, on their way to civilization. In our
study of humanity, the lower races of men are as
essentially important as the higher; our present
higher races being but the lower types of generations yet to come. The nations now most civilized
were once barbarians. Our ancestors were savages,
who, with tangled hair, glaring eyes, and blood-
besmeared hands devoured man and beast alike."
From this point of view, does not a study of the
North American Indians become of great interest
to us?

The first knowledge we have of America or its
inhabitants, outside of the prehistoric, is derived
from various visits of the Norsemen, between the
years 994 and 1012. The origin of the native Indians is yet an unsettled question. It is my purpose to deal with them only from the beginning of
authentic history.

For the purpose of accounting for the change in
the character of the Indians from "quiet, peaceable
people," as they were always at first reported to be,
to what they were afterwards termed—savages,—I
may be permitted to cite a few facts in history

regarding the treatment they have received at the hands of the whites from their earliest acquaintance with them.

It is well known that when Columbus, upon his first voyage in 1492, discovered land, he supposed he had reached India by a western passage, and, finding the land inhabited by a race of people unlike any he had ever seen or heard of, he called them Indians —a name which has since remained the distinguishing cognomen of all the native inhabitants of America. He found them a quiet, peaceable people, as is shown by one of his biographers, Andres Bernaldez, an intimate friend under whose hospitable roof Columbus had often been entertained, both before and after his voyages. He informed Bernaldez that:

"These people were all simple, peaceable, liberal, and well-disposed, sharing with each other, making free with whatever they possessed, and giving without stint. Those that came to the ships, after they had recovered from their fears, showed toward our people much love and good-will; and for whatever was given them they returned many thanks and received it with much gratitude, and gave whatever they had in return. This was not in consequence of their simplicity or lack of understanding, for they are a very subtle race, of much acuteness, and they navigate all the neighboring seas, and it is wonderful to hear the account they give of everything, except that they never heard of people wearing clothes, or of such vessels as those of the Spaniards."

From this we may see what the native Indians

were, as they were found by Columbus, prior to any association with the "civilization of Europe"; and if, in our further contemplation of their character and habits, we find them changed, we may be able to fix the responsibility for such change where it rightfully belongs.

Upon the second voyage of Columbus, we find that *he* began treating these simple natives in a manner by no means in accord with the hospitality with which they had received him. His biographer says: "He made incursions into the interior and captured vast numbers of natives; and the second time that his vessels returned to Spain, he sent five hundred Indian men and women, all in the flower of their age, between twelve years and thirty-five, or thereabouts. They were delivered at Seville to Don Juan de Fonseca, and sold as slaves, but proved of little service, for the greater part of them soon died."

We see here the beginning of that inhuman and un-Christian conduct towards the Indian which has so changed his character.

In 1497 John Cabot, with his son Sebastian, visited the northern coast. They were more considerate or more modest than Columbus, for they only kidnapped three Indians, whom they took as curiosities to Henry VII. of England.

In 1500 Caspar Cortereal, a Portuguese admiral, sailed along the northeastern coast. "He returned," says his historian, "with glowing reports of the fruitfulness of the country in herbage and in trees fit for shipbuilding, and with a number of captive Indians, whom he sold as slaves."

Numerous voyages were made by Europeans to the New World between the last mentioned date and the permanent settlement of the country. Among these was that of Bartholomew Gosnold, in 1602, who reported in regard to the Indians found by him, that "these people are exceeding courteous, gentle of disposition, and well-conditioned."

Another voyage was that of George **Waymouth**, in 1605. Of the Indians he says: "When we came on shore they most kindly entertained us, taking us by the hand, and brought us to sit down by their fire. They filled their pipes, and gave us of their excellent tobacco as much as we would." One day two canoes, each carrying three Indians, came out to the ship, and three of the visitors were induced to go on board. What then happened is thus related by Waymouth: "Because we could not entice the other three on board, we gave them a can of peas and bread, which they carried to the shore to eat. When our captain was come we considered how to catch the other three at shore, which we performed thus: We manned the light boat with seven or eight men; the one standing in front carried our box of merchandise, as we were wont to do when we went to traffic with them, and also a platter of peas, which food they loved; but before we were landed one withdrew himself into the wood. The other two met us on shore to receive the peas, with whom we went up the cliff to their fire and sat down with them, and

while we were discussing how to catch the third man
who was gone, I opened the box and showed them
the trifles to exchange, thinking thereby to have ban-
ished fear from the other, and draw him to return ;
but when we could not, we used little delay, but
suddenly laid hands upon them, and it was as much
as five or six of us could do to get them into the
boat, for they were strong, and so naked that our
best hold was by the long hair on their heads. Thus
we shipped five savages and two canoes, with all
their bows and arrows."

This was the return they made for all the con-
fiding kindness and hospitality of these " savages."
Savages indeed there were ; but in this case, as in so
many others, they were not the red men !

In 1614 one Thomas Hunt, master of a vessel,
kidnapped twenty Indians at Plymouth and seven
at Cape Cod, whom he carried to Spain and sold as
slaves.

Thus we see that nearly every expedition visiting
their country returned the kindness and hospitality
of the Indians by kidnapping some of their number
and carrying them away from their kinsmen and
native land, to suffer and die among strangers, as
prisoners or as slaves. Is it any wonder that their
race, proud and unforgetting, should eventually turn
upon their wanton persecutors to wreak vengeance
for the wrongs they had suffered ?

Many attempts had been made to plant colonies
in the New World, but the permanent settlement of
this part of the country began with the Puritans,

who arrived off Plymouth, Massachusetts Bay, on the eleventh day of November, 1620, and made a landing for permanent settlement on December 22d. They found the Indians a peaceful and well disposed people, willing to aid and succor the new-comers to the extent of their ability, but shy and timid.

The Puritans numbered one hundred men, women, and children, out of which number fifty-one died during the first winter. Had the Indians been otherwise than friendly, they could have destroyed the little band of forty-nine very easily. But instead of offering them harm, Massasoit, the chief of the Wampanoags, in whose country the whites had settled, came voluntarily and made a treaty of peace with them, which this tribe kept sacred and inviolate for fifty-four years.

It must be remembered that America was inhabited by a great number of different tribes or nations of Indians (since ascertained to have been over four hundred), each tribe having a different name and language, and living entirely distinct and separate from the others, and not infrequently waging war, at the end of which the victors always laid the vanquished tribe under immediate tribute ; so that while one tribe was peaceful, another might be disposed to go on the war-path.

The Narragansetts (which, judging from their position on the coast, was the tribe from which Waymouth had captured his five " savages ") felt unfriendly, and one day their chief sent a bunch of newly made arrows, wrapped in a snake's skin, to the Puritan settlement. This was a notice of declaration of war. Although the Puritans had previous to this been reinforced to some extent by the arrival of a ship from England, they could not muster more than forty or fifty fighting men. But to show fear, meant annihilation for the entire settlement ; so they filled the snake's skin with powder and bullets, and returned it to the chief with this message : " If you want war, you may come whenever you like, and get your fill of it." The Indians were very much afraid of the " pooh-guns that smoke," as they called the muskets, and when the Narragansett chief saw that the "pale-faces" were not afraid, but showed fight, his respect for the "pooh-guns" deterred him from beginning the war.

In 1633, the whites had begun to enlarge the bounds of their settlements, and some had gone as far south and west as the Connecticut River, a distance of about one hundred miles. Here they found beautiful and exceedingly fertile lands, occupied by the Pequots. They wanted them ; and that seemed sufficient reason for taking any means necessary to get them.

In that year, the governor of Plymouth Colony, having heard these reports, sent a committee to examine the Connecticut River and its banks. This committee reported that the land was partially cleared and under cultivation by the Indians ; that the streams abounded in fish, and the forests in game ; that the fox, otter, beaver, wolf, bear, deer, and moose, with many other wild animals, held possession of the territory in common with the Indians; that immense flocks of pigeons tenanted the woods, and innumerable water-fowl the streams. After describing the character of the soil, timber, etc., they say :

" Providence led us to that place. It is indeed far away from our plantations, and the Canaanites and the Amalekites dwell in that valley, and if they have any attachment to any spot on earth, must delight to live there. But the land must be ours. Our people have strong hands and pious hearts, and can overcome all difficulties. Let us go and possess the land, and in a few years you will hear more boast in this colony, that that land is better for flocks and herds than could ever be justly said of the land of Goshen, or any part of the land of Canaan."

A short time after the reception of this glowing report, these men with " pious hearts " mustered all their forces, stealthily surrounded a large village of the Pequots, and surprised and completely massacred them in one night. The whites had it all their own way, and, when the morning broke, rejoiced their " pious hearts " in counting six hundred and ninety-five Indian men, women, and children weltering in their own blood.

This inhuman butchery so overawed the Indians, who had never known or dreamed of such fearful slaughter, that for many years no one of them dared lift his hand against a white man, no matter what the provocation might be ; and these men, who left the persecutions of the Old World that they might enjoy *liberty of conscience*, had no further trouble in settling upon the beautiful lands of the Pequots, without money and without price.

The Indians were denounced as cruel savages, but Mr. Willard, of Deerfield, Massachusetts, who wrote in 1790, says:

" The Indians committed no offences without provocation, their offences were always in retaliation ; and in comparison with the long black catalogue of crimes committed in Christian nations, but few are found to occur among Indians. Is ingratitude among the number of their sins ? The most eminent and glorious examples of the opposite are on record. Did Indians ever sell wooden nutmegs and cucumber seeds, horn flints, or imitation powder? Did the Indians ever hang a poor Mrs. Richardson, simply because she was a Quaker and differed from them in religious belief?

" The Pilgrim fathers were stern and hardy men, upon whose character so many of us delight to dwell, but that character suffers in some respects by a comparison with that of the sons of the forest, who had only the light of nature to guide them.

" Time has shown us that the longer the Indians reside in the vicinity of white men, the more vicious and corrupt they become, and that they were always the objects or subjects of the white man's fraud and imposition, and there can be little doubt that more acts of cruelty have been committed on this continent by the Spanish, French, and English, or by their instigation, than by the natives."

It may perhaps be said that the end to be attained justified this wholesale destruction of the Indians;

that it is better for the world to have civilization progress, even though it be by the annihilation of uncivilized races. But we must remember that in judging Indian character, and as to whether they were justified in acting as they have acted, we should look at all the events touching them through their eyes—from their point of view, not ours.

In 1660 Wamsutta, the successor of Massasoit, the chief of the Wampanoags, came into power, and, while returning to his home after a visit to the whites, and before he had left their settlements, sickened and died. His brother, Metacom, whom the whites called "King Philip," succeeded him as chief. King Philip was of the opinion that his brother had been poisoned, and this, added to the wrongs of the ever-increasing encroachments of the whites upon his lands, made him resolve upon revenge.

Knowing the fate of the Pequots, and that his tribe alone could not successfully fight the whites, he prevailed upon some of the surrounding tribes to make common cause with him, and when he thought the confederacy strong enough to annihilate the "pale-faces," he began the conflict known in history as "king Philip's war," on the 24th day of June, 1675. This war resulted in serious loss to the whites, and, as ever, great slaughter to the Indians—not less than a thousand of the Narragansetts being killed on one Sabbath afternoon. At another time, three hundred of the Nipmuck tribe were surprised near the falls of the Connecticut River, and every one killed. In the same year Major Talcott, of Hartford, massacred four hundred at one time, near that place. The whites adopted the rule of taking no prisoners, and killed every man, woman, and child that fell into their hands; King Philip was shot on the 12th day of August, 1676, and "his severed head sent to Plymouth, where it was mounted on a pole and exposed aloft on the village green."

This ended the war, and many Indians came in and surrendered themselves. The whites seized a dozen of the chiefs who had thus surrendered, and hanged or shot them in the presence of the populace, and shipped hundreds of other Indians who had surrendered with their chiefs to the West Indies to be sold into slavery, among the latter being the wife and little nine-year-old son of King Philip.

Professor John Fiske says: "While King Philip's war wrought such damage to the English, it was for the Indians themselves utter destruction. Most of their warriors were slain, and to the survivors the conquerors showed scant mercy. The Puritan, who conned his Bible so earnestly, had taken his hint from the wars of the Jews, and swept his New England Canaan with a broom that was pitiless and searching. Henceforth the red man figures no more in central or southern New England, and as an element of disturbance or a power to be reckoned with, he disappears forever."

In the South and West, however, the Indians still existed in great numbers. Let us, then, turn our attention in that direction, and see if they were receiving any kindlier treatment at the hands of the white settlers there.

CHAPTER II.

IN 1584 Sir Walter Raleigh fitted out two vessels and sent them to the New World. They landed at the Roanoke River, in Virginia, and after engaging in profitable trade with the Indians returned to England, reporting that they " found the native Indians so affable, kind, and good-natured, so innocent and ignorant of all manner of politics, tricks, and cunning, and so desirous of the company of the English, that they seem rather to be like soft wax, ready to take an impression, than anyways likely to oppose the settling of the English near them."

They did not, however, continue in this condition for any great length of time.

One of the most prolific sources of trouble between the Indians and the whites, pertaining to all the settlements to a greater or less degree, was the abuse by the white men of the native women. Before the advent of the whites, an Indian woman could roam the woods day or night with entire safety and freedom from molestation by any man. These women were comely in form and feature, and seemed to be very attractive to the white men ; and they were frequently abused, even to the extent of kid-

napping and keeping them in the settlements. This
led to many murders; for if an Indian's wife or
daughter was thus outraged and in revenge therefor
he killed a white man, the whites would in retaliation kill one or more Indians, to impress upon the
natives the idea that they could never kill a white
man without suffering retaliation in kind, regardless
of the provocation that caused them to do so. The
insults to the Indians were never taken into consideration. These acts were followed by their natural
consequence—an inveterate hatred on the part of
the Indians, leading to murder whenever opportunity
offered—so that when a white man fell into the
hands of the Indians he seldom escaped death.

One notable case of deliverance from death, which
has been described in prose and sung in poetry,
wherever the history of Virginia has been told, was
that of Captain John Smith, one of the leading men
of that colony. He was a man of great energy and
courage, and possessed a spirit of adventure seldom
excelled.

Not satisfied with remaining at the settlement, he
pushed on into the interior. This alarmed the Indians, giving them the impression that the whites
were seeking to overrun their entire country. He
was attacked and all his men were killed, he alone
being taken a prisoner to Powhatan, who was the
great head chief of all that section. Powhatan had
heard of Captain Smith, and knew he was one of the
great chiefs of the " pale-faces," so he was at a loss
to know what to do with him, having a fear that if

he put him to death the whites would wreak terrible vengeance upon his nation. He therefore kept him a prisoner for six weeks, treating him with great kindness. Finally, however, he determined that the captive must die, and gave his orders to that effect. Two of the warriors bound the prisoner's hands and feet and laid his head upon the rock. At a signal from the chief, two other warriors, each armed with the deadly war-club, stepped forward and stood grim and still at the head of the prostrate victim, awaiting the signal to deal the fatal blow.

At this moment a wild scream pierced the air, and Pocahontas, the beautiful daughter of Powhatan, a girl of thirteen years, flew to the captive, threw herself upon his prostrate form, and, staying the arm of one of the warriors with her own, laid her head upon that of the prisoner, so that if the blow fell it must be upon her own head.

Powhatan was dumbfounded. He dearly loved his little daughter; but he was a great chief, and his orders must be obeyed. After a moment's hesitation he took her by the hand and raised her to her feet, when, with tearful eyes, she implored her chieftain father to spare the captive's life. Her plea was most eloquent, and Powhatan listened in mute astonishment. When it was finished, and while the sobbing girl was clinging to his knee, her streaming eyes fixed on his, the chief gave the order to unbind the captive and return him to his people.

Pocahontas always remained a true friend of the "pale-faces," and twice, while yet in her "teens," she

stealthily informed the whites of attacks contemplated by the Indians, thus saving many lives.

The whites returned these acts of kindness by kidnapping her when she was about eighteen years old,
and carrying her a prisoner to the settlement, where
they kept her for two years, while they were endeav-
oring to make a treaty of peace with her father,
thinking he would the more readily yield to their
demands if they held his daughter in their power.

During this time Pocahontas, who had now become a beautiful woman, made the acquaintance of
Mr. John Rolfe, an English gentleman of some
wealth and position, and became engaged to marry
him.   Powhatan being informed of these facts vouch-
safed his consent, and upon their marriage concluded
a peace, although declining to attend the wedding
for fear of treachery on the part of the whites.   Mr.
Rolfe took his Indian bride to England, and Captain Smith, in a letter to Queen Anne, made known
the leading events in her life, and the Queen received
her at court with all the honor due to the daughter
of a king.   After remaining for some time she started
to return with her husband to her native land, but
sickened and died before leaving England, at the
early age of twenty-three.

The death of Pocahontas was a sad disappointment to the colonists, who had indulged the hope
that her marriage with one of their leading men
would secure a lasting peace with the Indians. Their
disappointment was also accompanied by a fear that
the Indians would seek to retaliate upon them for

her death, under the suspicion that she had been poisoned, a suspicion that the Indians always entertained when any of their people died suddenly while visiting the whites.

But it was of no poison known to the toxicologist that Pocahontas died. This royal daughter of the forest had loved Captain Smith ever since in her girlhood she had laid her head upon his to save him from death.

Her engagement and marriage to Rolfe were contracted in the belief that the man she loved and by whom she was beloved, was dead, and it was only during her visit to England that she learned that she had been deceived. The poison which ended her young life was that which comes of a broken heart.

In the parish register at Gravesend, where she died, may be seen the following entry:

" 1616, May 21, Rebecca Wrothe, Wyff of Thomas Wroth gent. a Virginia lady borne, here was buried, in ye chancell."

Pocahontas had been baptized and given the name of Rebecca.

The selfish fears of the colonists were groundless, however. The Indians kept the faith, and abstained from all hostilities for many years.

Several attempts were made to plant colonies in Pennsylvania; one by the Hollanders, or Dutch, in 1631; one by the Swedes in 1638; another by the Dutch in 1645; and finally the English succeeded in permanently establishing one in 1664.

The Dutch settlement on the Delaware, called by

2

them the "Valley of the Swans," was burned by the Indians. The cause of its destruction was peculiar. The arms of Holland painted on a piece of tin had been set up by the colonists. The glitter of this rude escutcheon had attracted the attention of an Indian chief, who, in his ignorance, took it to make a tobacco box. This act the settlers construed as an insult to their native country, and sought out and killed the offending chief. The honor of their country was vindicated, but the vindication proved most costly. The friends of the murdered chief watched for their opportunity and gained possession of the fort by despatching the guard while the settlers were absent at work. Upon the return of the unsuspecting whites in the evening, they were all massacred, and the buildings were burned.

When William Penn became the leading spirit of the English colony in 1683, he adopted a new policy in dealing with the Indians, which culminated in "the famous treaty that was never sworn to and never broken." By his policy the rights of the Indians were considered and respected, and by reason of his wisdom and honesty the people of Pennsylvania enjoyed unbroken peace for many years.

In writing home, Governor Penn said: "We have agreed that in all differences between the colonists and the Indians, six of each side shall end the matter. Do not abuse them, but let them have justice, and you win them."

This is the only instance we have on record in which the Indians were treated squarely and honestly by the colonists; and it furnishes a practical illustration of what might have been expected of them had they been thus treated in all cases.

It is unnecessary to adduce further testimony as to the disposition of the native Indians when the white man first came to settle among them. We have seen how Columbus found them in the West Indies, how the Puritans found them in New England, and how the other English settlers found them in Virginia and Pennsylvania. All concur that they were kind and peaceable, and disposed to be friendly with their visitors. We have seen that in New England it took but a few years of association with the Puritans to change their character entirely; that in Virginia wholesale massacres began after a contact of only twenty-six years; while in Pennsylvania all troubles ceased entirely after the just policy of Governor Penn was adopted. Is it possible for any doubt to exist as to where the responsibility lies for the change that has taken place in the character of the American Indians, and can we wonder at the change?

In 1608, which precedes by twelve years the settlement in New England of which we have spoken, Henry Hudson discovered the river which bears his name in what is now the State of New York, and sailed up as far as the forty-third parallel of north latitude. He sold this country, or such right as he had acquired in it, to the Hollanders, or Dutch, who in 1614 built a fort on the river, one hundred and fifty-five miles above its mouth, at Albany, and another on the island of Manhattan. The latter settlement, called by them New Amsterdam, is now the city of New York, the metropolis of the American continent. There was great controversy and some fighting over this country between the Dutch and the English, but it finally came permanently into the possession of the English.

They found the country thickly inhabited by Indians who constituted the Iroquois Confederacy, composed of five distinct nations or tribes. These were the Mohawks, the Oneidas, the Onondagas, the Cayugas, and the Senecas. At first the Indians treated the white settlers with great kindness, but in a few years troubles began between them similar to those which took place between the Puritans and the Indians in New England, and arising from like causes.

The Iroquois were very powerful, and were more advanced in civilization, if we may use that term, than the tribes around them. They had almost a perfect form of republican government, and exercised through their confederacy so much power as to hold many of the surrounding nations under tribute. They controlled a vast territory, and much of it was consequently at a great distance from their seat of government. In 1647 they could muster many thousand warriors, well armed and equipped.

I have lived near them many years, and have become familiar with and carefully collated and studied their ancient legends; and in this way I have acquainted myself with much relating to their history

and personal life that has not heretofore been
written.

The confederacy now under consideration was
called by the French " The Iroquois." The English
knew it as " The Six Nations," the number of tribes
having been increased by the coming in of the Tuscaroras, in 1715. They called themselves *Ho-de-no-
sau-nee*, that is, " People of the Long House," of
which the Mohawks guarded the eastern and the
Senecas the western door.

I have said that their ancient government was republican, in form and principle. There was a general council composed of representatives from the
different tribes in the confederacy, the number from
each tribe being fixed in accordance with the number
of persons therein, counting both men and women.
The Mohawks had nine, the Oneidas nine, the Onondagas fourteen, the Cayugas ten, and the Senecas
eight, making a council of fifty.

The government I am describing was that which
existed prior to the Tuscaroras being admitted into
the confederacy. These representatives were elected
by the *viva voce* votes of both the men and the
women of the tribe that sent them, and were always
selected indiscriminately from among the sachems
and chiefs of the tribe. The women were entitled
to vote upon the election of all officers.

This council elected a sachem as presiding officer,
who thus became the head sachem of the entire
confederacy. The laws made by the general council constituted the supreme code by which the

confederacy was governed. In their own tribe, the chiefs chosen as representatives to the general council constituted, with the other chiefs of the tribe, the national or tribal council, and their presiding chief was the head chief of the tribe. All the sachems and chiefs held their offices during life or good behavior. There were many other chiefs besides those mentioned. Each tribe was divided into eight clans, each clan having two head officers, a sachem and a chief, who constituted the medium through which all laws and orders were conveyed to the people, so that each tribe always had eight sachems and eight chiefs. The clans were named alike in every tribe respectively, Wolf, Beaver, Snipe, Hawk, Bear, Turtle, Deer, and Heron, and a picture or other representation of the animal or bird for which it was named was the " totem " of the clan.

It was the duty of the sachem to look after all matters pertaining to the state ; while the chief was supreme in time of war. In rare instances, by reason of great merit, both these offices were conferred upon one individual. But if a sachem took the war-path, he must resign his sachemship for the time being.

Where, even in these days of advanced civilization, will we find a higher or better type of representative government than that of the ancient Iroquois? Among them there was no periodic scramble for office ; no dividing of political spoils among the wire-pullers and " workers " of the successful party. Birth gave an advantage, but merit was the only consideration that secured the chieftaincies. It seems to me that some enlightened republics of to-day might well take a lesson in pure government from these untutored " savages."

The Iroquois had no written language, but passed their history, etc., from generation to generation by memorized tradition. They had a system of mnemonics to assist them in this. Every great event, in fact everything they thought of sufficient importance to remember, was associated with a belt or string of " wampum," and, strange as it may appear, they could, by looking at such a belt, rehearse with accuracy everything that occurred at the time that belt was first put into use. These wampum belts were made in different widths. Small shells were strung on strings of deer skin or sinew, and the strings woven together. The shells were of various colors, and their shade and position in the belt served to convey to the mind the ideas with which they were associated.

These tribes had made some progress in agriculture. The journal of De Nonville, who commanded a French expedition against the Iroquois in 1687, speaks of large villages, especially among the Senecas. He counted three hundred and twenty-four houses in four villages, and destroyed one million two hundred thousand bushels of corn, besides great quantities of beans, squashes, and other vegetables, in these four villages alone.

The Onondagas, being near the centre of the confederacy, or " Long House," were the council-fire keepers, as well as the custodians of the record belts of wampum. It was in their domain that the general councils were always held.

Although the tribes composing the confederacy covered a vast territory, the members of the council could be reached very quickly by means of a system of very fleet "runners," of great endurance. The trails of these runners through the forests were always most direct; and as the swift messengers were simultaneously despatched in all directions, only a very short time was required to convene a council.

The first thing in order at a council was to smoke the "calumet," or pipe of peace. This practice was symbolic among all the tribes upon the continent. It was a sign of friendship, and constituted a mutual pledge of amity. The bowl of the pipe was usually made of stone finely wrought, the stem was two and a half feet in length, made of some strong reed and decorated profusely with feathers and shells. The ceremony was opened by the head sachem, who took a few whiffs and then passed the pipe to the person next to him upon his left, who, after taking a few whiffs, passed it to the next upon his left, and so on around the circle, until it again came to the head sachem, who then quietly placed it upon the ground at his right side. If any one refused the calumet, his action demanded immediate explanation.

Councils were sometimes held in the special interests of the women of the confederacy. The women were the workers, who tilled the soil, dressed the skins, wove the wampum belts, and did all the household labor, but they were well treated. They had a voice in the choice of sachems and chiefs, and of themselves elected officers who were denominated "Women's Men," and whose duty was to look after and protect the interests of the women. If they desired to have any matter considered, they could call a council of their clan, and, if it was a matter of general interest, then a council of their tribe or nation ; and in case the opinion of the women of the other nations of the confederacy was deemed necessary, a general council was called to attend to their interests, as readily and quite as much as a matter of course as one for the consideration of matters in which the men were specially concerned.

The women were never admitted to the councils of the men, but in the councils for the women they were not only admitted, but called upon to represent their grievance, or to speak upon whatever subject the council had been called to consider. The men, however, decided the matter by a vote among themselves.

Marriages among the Iroquois were not always based upon affairs of the heart. There was a law among them inhibiting marriages between members of the same clan. Such were regarded as brothers and sisters, even though no blood relationship subsisted between them. The mothers were the " matchmakers," and sometimes acted without the slightest regard for the feelings of those most interested, though the maiden was usually consulted.

When a young man or maiden wished to marry, or when a mother desired a marriage for her son or daughter, the grandmother, if living, or, if not, the mother (or, when there was no grandmother or mother, the eldest female relative upon the mother's side), made the proposition by leaving a present in a basket at the door of the wigwam where the young man or maiden (whichever was to be wooed) resided. This gave notice to all that a marriage was contemplated. The relatives of a maiden could make the proposition to the mother of the desired young man with as much propriety as those of a young man to the mother of the maiden. If the proposition was agreeable, the basket was taken into the wigwam, and if its contents proved acceptable it was returned with a present, which action left the way open for further negotiations. But if the proposal was rejected, the basket would be left untouched, to be carried away by the one who brought it. This was a flat refusal. After the acceptance of the first present, the negotiator took a second of greater value, and entered the lodge herself and consulted with the women of the family with whom she sought an alliance. If all were in favor of the marriage, each family informed the son or daughter; after which a meeting of the women was arranged at which the young man and maiden would be present, and listen to serious advice concerning the respective duties of husband and wife.

The final ceremony of marriage was quite simple. A seat having been prepared in the wigwam of the bridegroom, the friends of the young people joined in a march from the house of the bride to that of the groom, and having arrived there the bride and groom, in presence of all the company, joined hands and seated themselves. This ended the ceremony.

In the case of second marriage the parties were at liberty to negotiate for themselves.

The fathers had no actual ownership of the children ; these belonged to the clan and tribe of the mother. If a marriage proved unhappy the parties to it were permitted by custom to separate at will and each was at liberty to marry again, but the mother had the sole right to the disposal of the children, and kept them all if she chose. She retained control also of whatever property belonged to her at the time of her marriage, and could dispose of it as she pleased without the husband's consent, either while living with him as wife or after separation.

As in other Indian tribes, the Iroquois man could have more than one wife if he pleased, but on account of the ease with which any marriage compact could be dissolved, this seldom happened. The Indian who valued the peace of his household knew better than to jeopardize it by the presence of two or more women standing in the same relation to him, and felt that his chance of comfort and happiness was far better with one at a time, in which he doubtless displayed much wisdom.

A missionary was once talking to one of these Indians in regard to the sin of such easy separation, and received from him this sententious reply : " You marry white woman ; she know you have to keep her always, so she scold, scold, scold, and no cook your venison ; I marry squaw ; she know I leave her if she no good, so she no scold, she cook my venison, and we live long happy together." It was his way of saying that the chain galls least that binds most lightly.

The Indian women were very affectionate—much more so apparently than the men. There is nothing an Iroquois mother would not do for her child, even to the sacrifice of her life ; and when she loved her husband, she would do anything or endure anything for him.

CHAPTER III.

THE Iroquois were very fond of dancing, always indulging in it as a part of their religious ceremonies, as well as upon festival occasions. Their religious dances were performed with slow and solemn tread, while their festive dances were in light and lively measure.

The great dance, however, which called forth all the energy, endurance, and enthusiasm of the performers, and threw them, as well as the spectators, into the wildest excitement, was the war dance. Every Indian nation indulged in it, but nearly every tribe had a different manner of executing this highly dramatic performance. That of the Iroquois gave free license to each individual to make himself as frightful in appearance as possible, and to illustrate any act of daring that might be conjured in his excited brain. None but the warriors took part in this dance, and each dressed himself in the most hideous costume (principally *paint*) that his fancy could devise, the leading idea being that his terrible appearance in battle would tend to fill his enemy with dismay, and thus make victory more easy. In this we see a close resemblance to those Old-World warriors of not many centuries ago, who covered their armor with the skins of wild beasts, leaving head and ears erect, and open mouths showing savage teeth to terrify the foe. The Indian added to this frightful make-up the blood-curdling war-whoop; and I will say, having had some experience in the matter, that if there is any sound on earth that will take the color from the white man's cheek quicker or more effectually than the war-whoop of the Indian breaking upon his waking ear, I have yet to hear it.

The dance itself was an imitation battle; arrows flew thick and fast; the tomahawk was wildly brandished on high to imitate its deadly work; each scalp suggested the death-struggle with its original possessor, and that struggle was all gone through with again in pantomime. By the effect of paint and scalps, the battle-field was covered with the dead and dying enemy. When the warriors had become nearly exhausted, at a signal from the chief the war-whoop was changed to the shout of victory, and all retired to partake of the feast prepared by the women for the mimic victors.

The Iroquois disposed of their dead by burial, but not until the body had lain for ten days upon a raised platform. During this time the relatives of the deceased kept a fire burning constantly near by and kept watch over the body. This was done for two reasons: *first*, that no one should be buried alive; and *second*, because these people believed that the spirit of the dead hovered around the body for

ten days after death, before taking its flight to the
happy hunting-grounds, and by this fire and constant
watch they expressed their affection. At the expi-
ration of the ten days, the body was buried. If it
were that of a woman, a plentiful supply of food and
all her kettles and cooking utensils were put into the
grave ; if that of a hunter, his bow and arrows ; and
if that of a warrior, his bow and arrows, tomahawk,
and scalping-flint. The body was always placed in
the grave in a sitting posture, which was the position
assumed by the listener at councils or gatherings of
any kind ; and as it was believed that the first thing
to be done on arrival in the spirit-land was to listen
to the counsel of friends who had gone before, the
newly buried one would thus be in the proper atti-
tude. Just as the body was being lowered into the
grave, a live bird was placed upon it and released, to
symbolize by its flight that the spirit of the dead
then took its flight to the spirit-land ; and, as it was
firmly believed that there the good were far more
happy than in this life, mourning for the dead ceased
with the burial, and the grief manifested thereafter
was for the loss the living had sustained in the re-
moval of their relative. When a chief died, the
burial ceremony was attended with great formality
and pomp.

The Iroquois firmly believed in a state of future
rewards and punishments, and that in the other
world the good are separated from the bad. Their
experience led them to look upon the whites as bad,
and they rejoiced in the hope and faith that they

should find there a blessed country which no white man's foot would ever be permitted to profane.

That desire was one thing that operated against the missionaries in their efforts to "convert" the Indians.

An old chief expressed the deep-seated feeling of his people when, solicited upon his death-bed to accept the Christian religion, he said : "No;—get white man's religion—then, when die, go where white man go—*no want to.*"

Their idea was that there was eternal life beyond the grave, and that friends would recognize each other in the next world the same as in this. They believed in one God, and that He made the earth and everything in it that was good, and they ascribed to Him all good. They also believed in an evil spirit, corresponding to the Biblical devil, who was ever going about doing evil. They attributed to this evil spirit creative powers also; believing that he created all monsters, snakes, and poisonous plants :—reasoning that a God who was all goodness would never have made anything that would harm His children. There was no religious division among them, and they had no need for priests or ministers; for they all worshipped the same God, and in the same manner. Their worship was a spiritual one; they had no idols. A post, or totem, set up in the centre of the village and occasionally in other places, and upon which were inscribed many records and hieroglyphics, was sometimes carved in representation of a grotesque face, arms, etc.; and this carving and the

veneration in which the posts were held led some of
the early historians to believe that they were idols.
But those who became acquainted with the language
found them to be merely totems, or record posts.

The Iroquois being a powerful and warlike people,
the nations of the Confederacy had many warriors
who, like the standing armies of to-day, were idle,
with no chance to win laurels unless engaged in
hostilities. The result was, that idleness bred rest-
lessness, for (except the war dance) they had nothing
of even the small relief afforded the soldier of the
present day by drills and manœuvres; whence they
were almost continuously engaged in war.

Their traditions tell us that their Confederacy was
formed a number of years prior to the settlement of
the white man on this continent. They also inform
us that the first contest of the Confederacy, in which
the warriors of the whole five nations joined forces
and fought side by side, was with the Eries, a large
and powerful tribe residing on the south shore and
at the lower end of the great lake that still bears
their name, their principal village being located near
what is now the city of Buffalo.

The Eries had learned of the formation of the
Confederacy and were greatly troubled thereby. So,
in order to find out whether the five nations would
really act together, they sent a challenge to them to
select one hundred of their most athletic young men
to meet a like number chosen from the Eries, in a
friendly game of ball for a wager. Upon receiving
this challenge, the Iroquois called the council to-

3

gether, and after some debate it was decided not to accept it, and a message to that effect was sent to the Eries. The challenge was sent a second time, and again declined. A third challenge was sent, and by this time the young men had become so excited that the older ones could not restrain them, and it was finally decided to accept the challenge. A hundred of the best players in the five tribes were selected, and under the leadership of an experienced chief and without arms, they went to meet the Eries, carrying with them a large quantity of costly wampum belts, beautifully ornamented moccasins, rich beaver robes, and other articles of great value in the eyes of the Indian, and which the Iroquois chief caused to be deposited in a pile on the field where the game was to be played. These were all carefully matched, piece by piece, by the chief of the Eries. The game was played with great vigor on both sides, but it became evident, almost from the start, that the Eries were over-matched, not only in skill but in the strength, swiftness, and endurance of the players, and the Iroquois triumphantly bore off the prize. This ended the first day.

On the following morning the Iroquois prepared for departure; but the Erie chief said that although they had been fairly beaten in the ball game, their young men would not be satisfied unless they could have a foot-race, and he proposed to match ten of their number against an equal number whom the Iroquois chief should pick from his party. This was finally acceded to, the runners were selected, the race was run amid much excitement, and the Iroquois were again the winners. This ended the second day.

Early on the morning of the third, the Iroquois started for home. But the chief of the Eries, not concealing his dissatisfaction with the result of the two contests, stopped them, and proposed as a final trial of skill, strength, and prowess, to select ten of his men to be matched against an equal number of picked men of the Iroquois in a wrestling match, and that the victor should dispatch his adversary on the spot with the tomahawk, and bear off his scalp as a trophy. This proposition was flatly refused by the Iroquois chief; but upon its being repeated, with taunts as to their lack of courage, the Iroquois decided to accept the sanguinary challenge, but determined in their own council that should they come off victorious they would not perform the last act called for by the proposition. A lithe, handsome Iroquois of the Seneca tribe first stepped forward, and, after a short but fierce struggle, laid his competitor upon his back. The chief of the Eries at once presented the victor with a tomahawk with which to brain his adversary, who lay prostrate at his feet. This he refused to do; but quick as thought, and with flaming eyes, the chief seized the tomahawk and buried it in the skull of his own warrior. The quivering body was quickly dragged aside, and another champion of the Eries presented himself.

He was a fine specimen of athletic manhood in the flower of youthful vigor, and in his dark eyes shone the baleful light of desperate determination; for he

knew that his only chance of life was to dash down
his adversary. The well-knit Iroquois who met him
quickly realized that it was no woman's arm that was
thrown around him in that embrace for life or death.
The Erie champion seemed to put his utmost strength
into his first effort to bear his antagonist at one dash
and by sheer force to the earth. The Iroquois, apparently not fully prepared for the sudden fierceness
of the attack, was forced quickly backward, even
while rigidly maintaining the firm arch of his powerful back. But he was still borne backward, despite of
all his strength, and seemed unable to recover himself. Hope revived in the faces of the Eries, while
those of the Iroquois party remained stolid and immovable, only their chief looked troubled. At this
point the Erie wrestler made a quick attempt to get
his right foot behind the heel of his backward-moving
adversary, and, by thus tripping him, end the struggle. Fatal attempt! The wiry Iroquois seemed
waiting for this; for, gathering himself with a supreme effort as the Erie's foot left the ground he
swayed his own powerful body quick as a flash to the
right, and with a slight backward movement laid the
Erie first upon his side and then flat upon his back.
Again the deadly tomahawk did its bloody work in
the hands of the infuriated chief, and the second
victim was dragged aside.

A third champion of the Eries stepped forward.
He seemed to have little confidence of success, and
looked like a man doomed to death. His athletic
antagonist quickly and easily twisted him to the

earth. Then the chief of the Iroquois sprang forward to intercede for the life of the vanquished warrior, but he was too late ; the Erie chief had killed his third champion. Then the Iroquois chief said there should be no more wrestling, and gave the signal for his warriors to retire ; and without further parley the victorious band turned their faces homeward. But on their dark faces a shadow rested—the shadow of life wantonly sacrificed.

The events of these three days convinced the Eries that it would be futile for them to cope with the aggregated strength of the confederated Iroquois, and fearing that they might soon be attacked by them, and knowing that their only hope was to destroy the tribes separately, they determined at once to raise a powerful war party and by a vigorous and sudden movement to surprise and destroy the Senecas, who were the nearest to them of the confederated nations.

There was living at this time among the Eries a Seneca woman who had been taken prisoner by them in her girlhood, and who, being adopted into the tribe, had married an Erie warrior who soon after died, leaving her without children. Seeing the extensive preparations for a bloody onslaught upon her own people, this brave and loyal woman determined to apprise the Senecas of their danger. Awaiting her opportunity, she stole away on a dark night and went down the Niagara River to the great Falls, and from there to Lake Ontario. Here she was so fortunate as to find a canoe drawn up on the beach, and launching it she coasted along the shore until she came to the mouth of a river, near which was a large village of her own people. Landing here, she made her way, footsore and weary, to the abode of the head chief, to whom she quickly made known the object of her visit.

Runners were dispatched at once to all the tribes, summoning their chiefs to meet in immediate council. When convened, the Seneca chief informed them of the intended invasion of the Eries, and all agreed that preparations must be made with all possible speed to meet the foe. A body of five thousand warriors was quickly got together, with a reserve of one thousand young men who had never been in battle. The head war-chief of the Confederacy took command, and spies were sent out ahead to look for the enemy. The main body of warriors had scarcely passed the last settlement of the Senecas when the spies returned, bringing word that the Eries were coming in great force, less than two days' march ahead.

The Eries had not the least suspicion of the approach of the Iroquois forces. They were relying upon the secrecy and celerity of their own movements to surprise and destroy the Senecas almost without resistance. The Iroquois formed in ambush, but were discovered, and the opposing forces met on the banks of a small stream. The Eries were greatly surprised at meeting the enemy under such circumstances, but nothing could daunt their courage or exceed their impetuosity. They rushed across the

stream and fell upon the Iroquois with tremendous
fury. The battle raged fearfully. No quarter was
asked or given on either side. The Eries were
proud, and had been victorious hitherto over all
their enemies. They knew how to conquer, but not
how to yield. On the other hand, the united forces
of the weaker nations, now made strong by union
and brought together for the first time as allies in
battle, fought with a spirit of emulation, excited to
the highest degree among the warriors of the different tribes. Though staggered by the first furious
onslaught of the Eries, they quickly rallied and made
a determined stand. Then the battle raged with
the utmost fury. The war-club, the tomahawk, and
the scalping-flint, wielded by powerful dusky arms,
each did its terrible work of death. Seven times
had the Eries been driven back across the stream,
and as many times had they regained their ground.
During the hottest of the fight the head chief of the
Iroquois executed a brilliant strategic movement.
The reserve of a thousand young men, who had not
yet shown themselves in the conflict, were, under
cover of the underbrush, massed on the other side of
the stream, in the rear of the Eries; and when the
latter were driven back for the eighth time, this fresh
reserve, at a signal from their leader, rushed with a
tremendous yell upon the now almost exhausted
Eries, and quickly decided the fortunes of the bloody
day. The victors gave their enemies no rest, but
pursued them in their flight until they were almost
entirely annihilated. Only a few swift runners and

stragglers of the vanquished Eries escaped to carry
the news of their terrible defeat to the women and
children and the old men who remained at home.

After thus conquering the Eries, the confederated
nations took possession of their territory, which
brought them in contact with the Hurons. Having
learned their power, they from this time forward inaugurated a campaign of conquest, and did not rest
until they had subdued many of the nations as far
west as the Mississippi River. On the south they
extended their conquests to the Gulf of Mexico ;
on the north to Hudson Bay ; and on the east to the
Atlantic Ocean. This left them the masters of an
immense territory—the finest on the continent.

This was the condition of the Iroquois when the
whites first settled here ; and it so remained until
they took sides in the wars between the French and
English, and later between the English and American colonies. The tribes they had conquered merely
paid them tribute in corn and skins, which added to
their wealth and ease of living, but not to their
strength.

The steady and rapid encroachments of the white
men soon took from them the greater portion of the
soil which was their natural heritage, and penned
them up on reservations. As has been forcibly and
truly said of them : " The infectious air of civilization penetrated to the remotest corner of their
solitudes. Their ignorant and credulous nature,
unable to cope with a superior race, absorbed only
its worst features, yielding up their own simplicity

and nobleness for the white men's vices, diseases, and **death."** They are now reduced to about seven thousand, and are much scattered, living on various reservations in the United States and Canada.

There were but two roads to distinction among the Iroquois—one war, the other oratory. They held their oratorical sachems in great honor. The one best known and most celebrated among the whites was *Sa-go-ye-wat-ta*, meaning " He keeps them awake." He was known among the whites as " Red Jacket," having received that name from the fact that an English officer had once given him a red coat, which Red Jacket always wore on great occasions and of which he was very proud. He was a man of great ability and remarkable powers of oratory. He was born in 1750, and was on the stage of action during the trouble between England and the colonies. He always opposed the Indians' taking up the hatchet on either side. He foresaw the destruction of his people, and thought the taking up of arms upon behalf of the white man's quarrel would hasten that destruction. He had noted how they were being surrounded by civilization, and wasting away, and in one of his speeches, alluding to this condition, he said :

" We stand upon a small island in the bosom of the great waters. We are encircled—we are encompassed. The Evil Spirit rides upon the blast, and the waters are disturbed. They rise, they press upon us ; and the waves once settled over us, we disappear forever. Who then lives to mourn for us?

None. What marks our extermination? Nothing.
We shall be mingled with the common elements."

On another occasion, addressing an assemblage of
whites, he said :

" Your forefathers crossed the great water and
landed upon this continent. Their numbers were
small. They found friends, and not enemies.
They told us they had fled from their own country
on account of wicked men, and had come here
to enjoy their religion. They asked for a small
seat. We took pity on them and granted their request, and they sat down among us. We gave them
corn and meat ; they gave us ' fire water' in
return."

Red Jacket died in 1830, and was buried in the
Indian burial-ground near the city of Buffalo, New
York. In 1884—the city having spread beyond this
little patch of ground, sacred only to the Indians—
the owners of the adjacent property bought the land
and had all the bodies removed. Some citizens,
thinking that Red Jacket deserved more than an unknown grave, had his remains reinterred in the beautiful cemetery known as " Forest Lawn," and a fine
bronze monument erected to his memory, at a cost
of ten thousand dollars.

Another of their orators was *Tah-gah-jute*, called
"Logan" by the whites. He had always advised
his nation not to join either side in the war between
the whites. His wigwam was known far and near
as the abode of hospitality, friendship, and kindness.
Although a Cayuga, he married a Shawnee woman,

and went to live with her tribe in the west. His wigwam was upon the bank of the Ohio River, near where the city of Wheeling, West Virginia, now stands, and there also he became a great favorite with the white settlers. He had always declared he would never lift his tomahawk against the white man. It happened, however, that in the spring of 1774 a difficulty arose between the whites and Indians in that section of country. It was called " Cresap's war." Logan remained quietly at home joining neither side. Colonel Cresap with a company of armed settlers, while on their way to join other forces that were gathering to fight the Indians, camped for the night not far from Logan's home. Some of the party wanted to do an act of daring to show their courage and immortalize their names, and therefore they set out during the night for Logan's wigwam. It did not matter to them whose it was ; it was enough to know that it was an Indian's. Logan was not at home, and they in cold blood murdered his two younger brothers, his wife, and all his little ones, and left them weltering in their blood upon the floor of his cabin. Logan returned in the morning to find his home tenanted only by the dead ; and then at once, for the first time, thirst for vengeance filled his soul, and from that moment he became the settlers' deadly foe. He immediately joined the Indians and fought for revenge, not only in the " Cresap war," but also during the early part of the long and bloody war between England and the colonies (called the Revolutionary war), filling the land with mourning.

When the war ended and the Indians were conquered, Logan was the last chief to sign the treaty
of peace, and he signed then only upon the earnest
solicitation of all the other chiefs. While before the
commission on this occasion he rose slowly from his
seat, and, with unspeakable sadness depicted upon
his countenance, spoke the following words :

"I appeal to any white man to say if ever he
entered Logan's cabin hungry, and he gave him no
meat ; if ever he came cold or naked and he clothed
him not. During the course of the long and bloody
war between the whites, Logan joined neither side,
but remained in his cabin, an advocate of peace.
Such was my love for the whites, that my countrymen pointed as they passed, and said Logan is the
friend of the white man. Colonel Cresap, in cold
blood and unprovoked, murdered all the relations of
Logan, not even sparing my wife and children. There
runs not a drop of my blood in the veins of any
living being. This called on me for revenge. I
have sought it. I have killed many. I have fully
glutted my vengeance. For my country I rejoice
at the beams of peace. But do not harbor a thought
that mine is the joy of fear. Logan never felt fear.
He would not turn on his heel to save his life. Who
is there now to mourn for Logan ? Not one."

When he had finished this pathetic address he sank
down upon his seat, a picture of despair; and, covering his face with his hands, wept bitter, scalding tears.
Then, recovering his composure, he arose majestically,
signed the treaty, and strode from the place.

There are several conflicting accounts as to when, where, and under what circumstances Logan made this speech, but all agree that it was made by him.

Up to the time of the slaughter of his family, Logan could not be induced to taste spirituous liquor; but after signing this treaty he sought relief from sorrow in the mind- and soul-destroying cup, and the great orator and noble-hearted man became a wreck.

He died in 1780, and a fine monument is erected to his memory near Sandusky, Ohio.

I have dwelt thus at length upon the Iroquois, because (excepting, perhaps, the Aztecs, in Mexico) their history is better known than that of any other nation upon the continent, because they exercised sovereignty over a vast territory, and because they are in many respects a type of most of the other Indians north of the thirty-third parallel of north latitude.

CHAPTER IV.

LIKE all unenlightened people, the Iroquois had many superstitions. One of the strongest of these was the significant importance which they attached to dreams. So great was this, that if any one had a clearly defined dream it was believed that it must be realized if possible, or dire calamity would follow. One illustration of the strength of this superstition will suffice :

Sir William Johnson, an English baronet, had settled among the Mohawks, and held wonderful sway over the Iroquois. He had a fine coat, highly ornamented and decorated, to impress the Indians with his greatness. This he wore on all state occasions. One day the head chief of the Mohawks, *Soi-en-ga-rah-tah*, who, on account of his great power and influence, was called by the whites "King Hendricks," came to Sir William and told him he had dreamed that Sir William gave him that coat.

Sir William, having lived long among them and well knowing that to obstruct the realization of the chief's dream would greatly weaken his influence among the Indians, immediately gave him the coat. Not long afterwards Sir William sent for the chief

and informed him that he had just had a remarkably
vivid dream to the effect that the chief had given
him such and such lands, naming a valuable tract
containing some three thousand acres. The chief
saw at once that he was beaten at his own game, and
for a moment hung his head. Then, slowly raising
his eyes, which had in them a little twinkle, he said :
"Well, Sir William, I will give you the land ; but
don't dream again !"

This chief joined the English in the war with the
French, and was killed in battle in 1755, when he
was about seventy years of age.

After the death of "King Hendricks," Joseph
Brant, whose Indian name was *Tha-yen-dah-na-gea*,
was, although not in the direct line of succession,
made by universal consent the head chief of the
Mohawks. He was born in 1742, and while a young
boy was taken in charge by Sir William Johnson.
At the age of thirteen he took part in the battle of
Lake George, where the French under Baron Dieskau
were defeated by the English forces under command
of Sir William Johnson. Brant also accompanied
Sir William in many expeditions against the French
during this war. He was placed in school by Sir
William at Lebanon, Connecticut, where he received
an English education. Later he took part in the
war with Pontiac and the Ottawas, and for many
years after this led a quiet life, as secretary to Sir
William and also to Sir Guy Johnson, who succeeded
to the agency after Sir William's death.

When the war broke out between the American

colonies and Great Britain, Brant adhered to his
patron, Sir Guy Johnson, and, with as many Mohawks as he could induce to go with him, joined the
British.   In the fall of 1775 he was commissioned a
captain in the British army, and went to England
for a personal interview with the officers of the home
government. He was there an object of much interest and at times attracted great attention by
appearing in full native costume, elegantly made,
and decorated in the height of ·Indian fashion.   On
his return to America, he entered actively into the
war, fully espousing the British cause, and urging
upon his people the ill-treatment the Iroquois had
received at the hands of the colonists.   The latter
used every endeavor to induce Brant to join them,
as did the English to retain him.   He was told by
the colonists that the king would surely be beaten,
as he had to bring all his soldiers across the great
water ; and that when the British were driven out,
as they were sure to be, the colonists would drive
him and his people from the country, in case he
adhered to the cause of Great Britain.

On the other hand he was told by Sir Guy Johnson that the king was rich and powerful, both in
money and subjects ; that his rum was as plentiful
as the water in Lake Ontario, and his men as numerous as the sands upon its shore ; that if he and his
people would persist in their friendship for the king
till the war was over, they would never want for
goods or money.   The bargain was struck with the
British, and each warrior was presented with a suit

of clothes, a brass kettle, an iron tomahawk, a scalp-ing-knife, and a small sum of money.

Brant at once became the chief commander of the Indian forces of the British in the east, and terrible indeed was the work done by him. When personally present, he was humane to prisoners. At the battle of Springfield, near Otsego Lake, in the State of New York, after capturing the town and killing or taking prisoners all the men, he collected all the women and children in one house and left them un-harmed, while he caused all the other buildings to be burned.

There are many conflicting reports and opinions as to the humanity or cruelty of this great chief. As the leader of the Indians upon the side of the British, he was of course blamed for all the massacres that took place, whether he had any personal knowl-edge of them or not; and in many instances it is im-possible to determine whether he was present or not. It is equally impossible to decide upon the truth or falsity of many of the stories that have been told, because of the excitement and prejudice that existed at the time. It is, however, beyond contradiction that in many instances the lives of women and chil-dren were spared by his efforts; and it is fair to pre-sume that he thus acted in all cases where he was personally present. He was unquestionably a man of great courage and ability.

After the close of the war of the Revolution, he left the United States and went into Canada with his followers, settling upon lands given them by the

4

British Government, and died there in 1807. A fine monument has been erected to his memory in the city of Bradford, in the province of Ontario.

The dress of the Indian, prior to the advent of the whites, was made entirely of the skins of animals, tanned with the hair or fur on or off, as best pleased the wearer. Some of their garments consisted merely of the tanned skin of some animal, wrapped around the body ; while others were regularly cut out and sewed together in the shape and style desired. The needles used for this purpose were fishes' bones, and the thread, when fine, was from the inner bark or roots of some tree, and when coarse, was cut from deer or elk skins or made from the animal's sinew. Some of these garments were quite pretty. They had an unique way of ornamenting them with bright-colored porcupine quills and shells, sometimes inter-mingled with colored grasses and feathers. They understood to a considerable extent the art of dye-ing in brilliant colors, principally the various shades of red, green, and yellow. Red was their prime favorite. They also showed considerable skill and taste in blending and harmonizing the colors which they used.

They were well skilled in the art of tanning, and spent much time in the process of scraping and rub-bing the skin over round sticks and between the hands, thus making it as soft and pliable as cloth. All work of this sort was done by the women. This mode of dressing and ornamenting skins was com-mon to all the Indians upon the continent, showing that with them, as with other races of men, necessity was the mother of invention, and that among all races similar circumstances suggest similar action.

Since the coming of the whites, and more particularly in sections where game has become scarce, the clothing of the Indian has been in great measure changed to cloths, blankets, and flannels. Beads of all colors have taken the place of porcupine quills, shells, etc., for ornamentation.

The women had entire charge of the children from birth to marriage, and they were kindly cared for. They had nothing to do but amuse themselves, until they became of sufficient age—the boys to accompany their fathers in the chase, and the girls to help their mothers.

When a young man arrived at the age of twenty, he might marry, provided he had secured by his own efforts—or his father would provide him with—sufficient skins, bows and arrows, canoes, or other property for acceptable wedding presents to the family of the bride. Girls were marriageable from about fourteen years of age ; and as it cost the young man nothing to furnish meat by hunting—a source of pleasure and amusement to him,—and his wife would raise all the corn and vegetables, besides dressing the skins and making the clothing, it was a very easy matter for the young man to support a family ; whence nearly all married at an early age.

The pappoose-board, or cradle, was made in various ways, the most common being a straight board about two and a half feet long, fifteen inches wide at the

top and nine inches at the bottom, made from cedar
or some other wood that would split straight and
easy. It was worked down with stone scrapers and
ornamented with paint to suit the more or less artistic
taste of the mother. Over the top was a hoop, under
which the infant's head was placed. The little one
was wrapped in furs and skins like a mummy, its tiny
arms bound close to its body with the wrappings.
Then this baby bundle was laid upon its back on the
board and fastened by lashings passed through holes
near the edges of the board and firmly laced. The
hoop over the top was to protect the head of the
child from bruises, in case the cradle should fall. The
cradle with its baby load was carried by the mother
upon her back, a strap made of woven bark or tanned
skin passing across her forehead and having the ends
fastened to the board. When the mother was at
work at home she would stand the cradle up against
the side of the wigwam ; but when working in the
field it was hung on a convenient bough of a tree, out
of reach of the wolves. This was an easy matter for
her, for all Indians could climb like squirrels, and the
infant being upon her back, held only by the strap
about her own head, did not interfere in the least
with her climbing.

I have seen from one to half a dozen or more specimens of this kind of fruit hanging upon a single tree,
while the mothers were picking berries. Strange as
it may seem, these children seldom cry, neither are
they easily frightened. Should you approach one of
them he would fasten his keen black eyes on yours

for an instant and then turn to his mother, if she were near, keeping his eyes vibrating between his mother and the stranger, but showing no signs of fear. If the mother was not present, the child would keep his little eyes continually fixed on yours with a gaze of intense interest. The child is kept upon the board for several months, or until his legs are strong enough to walk. Possibly it is this treatment that gives the Indian so erect a figure—a characteristic so universal as to justify the familiar phrase "straight as an Indian."

The country west of that occupied or overrun by the Iroquois was occupied by numerous tribes of Indians and quite thickly peopled to the Rocky Mountains, which formed a dividing line between these Indians and the tribes of the Pacific Coast.

The settlement of the white men among these Indians was attended with atrocities similar to those which characterized their advent among the Indians in the East, and to such an extent that murder became the seeming pastime of both races ; and to go into the details of it would be but to repeat, with slight change of circumstances, what has already been narrated concerning the Atlantic Coast. I shall therefore confine myself to the character, habits, beliefs, etc., of these tribes.

We learn from their traditions that before the white settlers came there were at different times among these Indians confederations similar to the great confederation of the Iroquois. Some of these were in fact still in existence when the whites first appeared.

They had some valiant leaders. Among those
known to history were Tecumseh, Black Hawk, and
Keokuk. In person, the men who inhabited this
section of the country were of large frame, compactly
built, and very muscular. The women, too, were large
and well formed, as befitted the consorts of such
men. As far as can be ascertained, these people
prior to the advent of the whites were humane in
their treatment of prisoners of war, some being
adopted into the tribe and others held as slaves.
The oldest man could remember of but one prisoner
who was burned at the stake, and that was said to
have been in retaliation for a like treatment of one of
their warriors taken prisoner by the whites down in
the southern country.

It is exceedingly difficult to locate the various
tribes as they were in the olden times. Some, who
were very powerful at one time in certain regions,
were overpowered and driven from their lands, to
settle in some distant section, there to become strong
again, and perhaps make conquest of neighboring
tribes. Owing to this uncertainty of location, it will
be more satisfactory to treat of these Indians in the
main collectively, although in some points the tribes
differed widely from each other.

The Shawnees with other tribes at one time occupied what is now the State of Ohio. It was among
this tribe that Simon Kenton, a celebrated scout,
had a remarkable series of adventures.

Kenton, at the age of seventeen, fled from Virginia to Kentucky, the then " Far West," to escape

punishment for killing his rival in the affections of a country belle. During the war of the Revolution he was employed as a scout, and performed some very daring deeds. At one time he was sent into the country of the Shawnees to ascertain their position and numbers. This he accomplished by going to their villages under pretence of being a friend, smoking the pipe of peace, and receiving their hospitalities. After thus obtaining all the information that was required, he started to return with his report. He had with him two friends who were bold and adventurous spirits, ready for anything that might come up. On their route they fell in with a few Shawnees who were keeping guard over quite a large herd of horses. Kenton suggested that they capture the entire herd and drive them home as a rich prize. This was readily agreed to, and the Indians, entirely unsuspecting, were quickly disposed of.

Some of the horses were then caught as leaders, and Kenton's comrades started off at good speed, while he drove up the laggards from the rear. They made directly for the Ohio River, dashing forward during the entire night without a halt. In the morning they stopped on a fine prairie where there was plenty of grass, to let the horses graze and rest a little. Setting out again, they travelled all that day and the following night, reaching the river far in advance of any pursuit. But the wind was blowing almost a hurricane, and they found the water so rough that with their utmost efforts they could not force the horses to swim the river. Hoping that their pursuers would not reach them before the waters subsided, they lay down on the bank to wait. But during the twenty-four hours of this enforced halt, the Indians in swift pursuit were covering the ground the whites had traversed the day before, and came upon them in the early morning.

Kenton's gun missed fire, and he took to the woods. He was hotly pursued, however, and soon made prisoner. One of his friends was killed, but the other succeeded in making his escape. The Indians fastened Kenton to a tree, calling him a thief, a horse-stealer, and a rascal; and he knew their language well enough to comprehend the force of these choice epithets.

In the morning the party started on their homeward march. For their amusement the Indians bound Kenton upon the back of an unbroken colt in real Mazeppa style, while at night he took his rest lashed to a tree as before. It took three days to reach their first village, where they bound him to a stake to be burned. They danced around him till midnight, whooping, yelling, and striking him with their hands and with switches; but for some reason unknown to him they did not apply the torch.

The next morning they unbound the captive, and, stripping him entirely naked, made him "run the gauntlet" between two rows of men and boys armed with switches, clubs, tomahawks, and other convenient implements of torture. At the end of the double row of Indians, which was about a quarter of a mile in length, stood the council-house, while at its entrance was an Indian beating a rude drum ; and it was understood that if the prisoner could escape the weapons and get into the house he was to be safe for the time being. This Kenton succeeded in doing, greatly to the astonishment of his captors. But his troubles were by no means ended. His offence had been too great to warrant his receiving any mercy. He had killed three or four of the Shawnees, and, what was nearly as bad, had stolen their horses, after smoking with them the pipe of peace and partaking of their hospitality.

On that day the Indians held a council to vote upon the question whether they should burn the prisoner at the stake there and then, or take him around and exhibit him in the other villages. The chiefs and warriors seated themselves in a ring and passed a war-club from one to another. Those in favor of enjoying the fireworks immediately were to strike the ground with the club before passing it, while those whose generosity inclined them to give the other villages the benefit of the exhibition were to pass the club in silence. Never was a candidate so interested in the vote of any club as was Kenton in the progress of this one. He watched it with eager eyes, and breathed freer when he counted a majority in favor of putting him on exhibition. It was not a cheerful prospect at best, but he knew this would give him at least a few more days—perhaps weeks—of life.

They put a rope around his neck, and led him thus

from village to village, the time occupied being
nearly a month.   At each village he was obliged to
run the gauntlet for the entertainment of the people,
and was vigorously switched on each occasion.   In
fact, during that month it may be said that running
the gauntlet was his chief occupation.   He did not
find it nearly so pleasant as killing a rival lover,
shooting Indians, or stealing horses.   Even scouting
would have pleased him better.   While sitting in the
council-house of one of the villages, after having had
his usual daily "run," and in expectation that the
next thing would be to bind him to the post for
burning, a white man came in with some prisoners
and scalps.   This proved to be the famous outlaw,
Girty, who had deserted the whites and joined the
Indians, and who excelled the latter in brutality and
savagery.   But he knew Kenton.   In former years
he had been a spy with him, had shared the same
dangers and slept under the same blanket with him.
That was enough ; and Girty, brute and traitor as
he was, began at once to plead for the life of his
friend.   In this he succeeded so far as to get him a
respite of three weeks, during which time Kenton
lived with him.   At the end of the three weeks, and
on the arrival of some other Indians from another
branch of the tribe, another council was held, and
even Girty's pleadings were in vain.   It was determined to take the prisoner to Sandusky, and there
burn him.   On arriving at the place of execution,
however, an English Indian agent interceded in
Kenton's behalf,—simply for the purpose, as he

alleged, of getting information from him for the British commandant at Detroit, and promising to return the prisoner as soon as he had accomplished that object.

The Indians finally, with great reluctance, gave Kenton into the agent's charge, who sent him immediately to Detroit. From there, by aid of an Indian woman, the wife of an English trader, he escaped; and by travelling by night and lying quiet during the day he reached his home in Louisville, Kentucky, in thirty days. Kenton lived to be eighty-two years old and to see the country over which he was dragged a prisoner covered with the farms and dotted with the towns and cities of the white man.

Among the tribes in this section were, besides the Shawnees, the Hurons, Algonquins, Assiniboins, Sioux, Apaches, Ojibways, Pawnees, Cheyennes, and Arapahoes. These tribes differed considerably from the Iroquois in their religious beliefs and in their dances.

Some of them believed that after death the spirit had to cross a deep and rapid river to reach the happy hunting-grounds; and that over this stream, as the only means of crossing, the Great Spirit had placed a very long pole, which the current kept in rapid and irregular motion. Those who had led good lives on earth were enabled to walk across in safety; while those who had been wicked would be shaken off and carried down the surging stream and over a high precipice extending between the hunting-grounds of the good and those of the wicked, and separating them for ever. The place reserved for the good was provided with every conceivable thing that could conduce to joy and happiness; while the wicked were condemned to live for all time in discomfort and misery.

They did not, like the Iroquois, ascribe creative powers to the Evil Spirit, although they believed that he exercised great power over their destinies and every-day life. But in their belief everything had a spirit—the corn, the apple-tree, the cave, the water, the wind, the thunder, the lightning—all were possessed of their especial spirit; and the Indians burned incense or made sacrifices to appease or propitiate each one, as circumstances dictated. They prayed only to the Evil Spirit; believing that the Good God would always befriend them without being asked or even thanked.

Their war dance differed materially from that of the Iroquois. Instead of imitating a battle, they set up a great post, and the warriors formed in a circle around it. Then one of them, painted as for war, would rush to the post, strike it with his whip or coup-stick, and in a loud voice relate his individual experience, exhibit the scalps he had taken, and in pantomime go through the struggle with each victim precisely as it had originally occurred. If in any part of the ceremony the performer should exaggerate, or lie, any one present who knew he was doing so was at liberty to step forward and throw dirt in his face, thus symbolizing that he ought to hide his face in shame for being guilty of such an offence.

This custom had the effect of keeping enthusiastic young warriors generally within bounds in the relation of their deeds of daring. On the other hand, if any warrior had achieved so many victories and had so many scalps that, to relate all his adventures would take too much time, the chief who had been selected to act as master of ceremonies would go to the post and place his hand over the mouth of the warrior, who would then at once retire. Such an act on the part of the chief was esteemed a great honor, for it bore eloquent though silent testimony that the warrior had performed so many valiant deeds that to recount them all would not only consume too long a time, but also tend to abash the younger warriors, whose showing would appear so meagre in comparison with his. The exhibition of scalps was an evidence of prowess that could not be disputed. The ceremonies of the dance were always followed by a great feast.

The tribes of this section indulged in a great variety of dances, some of them having different names for the same dance. Among them were the Scalp Dance, Medicine Dance, Green-corn Dance, Sun Dance, Begging Dance, Sign Dance, Eating Dance, Kissing Dance, and many other social dances. The social dances were attended with great merriment.

CHAPTER V.

THE Sioux, or Dakotas, as they sometimes called themselves, occupied the northwestern part of the country last described. They were numerous and powerful. Their numerical strength was, in 1846 (as stated by General Pike), 21,675, of whom thirty-eight hundred were warriors; and it is claimed by them that they were formerly very much more numerous.

It is the opinion of some writers that the Sioux belong to a race distinct from any other upon the continent; this view being based upon the evident difference in their physiognomy and language from those of all other known tribes; as well as upon their supplications and sacrifices to the " Unknown God," their meat- and burnt-offerings, and their preparation and burning of incense. I merely make this statement, without any intention of discussing it; my purpose being simply to give an account of the Indians as I found them.

Wild horses were plenty in this section of the country, and most of the tribes were expert horsemen and generally fought on horseback. This accounts for their custom of striking the post with their whips in the war dance, indicating the insult to an enemy, which will be spoken of hereafter. Instead of the tomahawk, these warriors used a lance as their principal weapon, keeping the tomahawk at their belts to be used in case the lance should be broken or when they came into close quarters.

The dress of all the tribes in this section was quite similar to that of the Iroquois, except that the men of rank wore a singular cap made of soft deer skin, fitting the head quite closely and having a pendant or tail extending down the back to the heels. This pendant was made in two pieces, and between these were fastened feathers, long ones at the head and others of gradually decreasing length to the heel. Fighting as they did on horseback, such an appendage was not burdensome, and this peculiar head-dress was often worn in battle when the rest of the body was covered only with paint. It was a matter of rejoicing if one of these caps was taken with a scalp, for it indicated that the wearer had been a man of importance.

To the Indian warrior an enemy's scalp, taken in battle, was what a captured flag is to the soldier of "civilized warfare,"—a proud trophy of his valor. Before scalping-knives were furnished them by the white traders, the Indians cut the scalp from the head of a vanquished enemy with a sharp flint. It was a feat requiring great prowess, for the victorious warrior during the time he was removing it remained exposed to onslaughts of the enemy,—it being one of the sacred tenets of all tribes never to let the body of a slain warrior fall into the hands of the enemy if they could prevent it. Whenever one of their number was seen to fall, others rushed immediately upon the victor to prevent his getting the scalp, whence the taking of it required great dexterity as well as courage,—both of which qualities were held in the highest estimation by all Indians. It is by no means strange, then, that the best evidence of a warrior's prowess was the number of these ghastly trophies in his possession.

With some of the tribes, however, there was a further reason for scalping an enemy. This was the belief that the loss of the scalp destroyed the immortal part, and secured the eternal annihilation of him from whom it was taken ; and thus by scalping their enemies here, they would have just so many the less in the other world.

Another belief prevailing to some extent among them was that the dead entered the other world exactly as they left this, and for that reason they wished to be dressed in their finest clothes when they died. It was thought also that every one who died would bear his wounds or deformities into the other world ; and this was why they sometimes refrained from scalping a slain white man, filling his body with arrows instead ; in the belief that, not being scalped, he would go into the other world, where he would be eternally tormented by the wounds the arrows had caused. This we would regard as a reckless waste of ammunition, but to them it appeared a wise provision for the future life.

Another curious custom, for the following of which the warrior would be highly honored, was that of striking the dead body of an enemy with the coup-stick or whip. This was regarded as a taunt and an insult, and the most strenuous exertions were made to prevent it. For this reason it was that in battle each side endeavored always to get the bodies of their slain beyond the reach of the enemy. One of the most dreaded calamities which could befall a tribe was the necessity that would compel them to leave any of their dead in the hands of their hated foes.

Feathers plucked from the wings of the war eagle were worn by all warriors in their caps or hair. They also tied them in the foretop and tail of their horses. Those worn upon the head were painted or cut in such a manner as to signify certain events, so that much of a warrior's record could be read upon his head. For example, the number of feathers with a spot of black paint upon them indicated the number of enemies he had slain; those with a V-shaped notch cut in the long side of the feather, the number of scalps he had taken; those split through the centre, how many times he had been wounded; those with three notches cut in the top, how many times he had insulted the enemy by striking the dead bodies of their warriors; while others, cut in various ways, indicated other daring exploits. The marked feathers occupied the most conspicuous place, while plain ones were used to fill out this fantastic head-dress, according to the taste of the wearer. Possibly it is this ancient custom of the Indian that originated

5

the familiar expression : " That puts another feather in your cap."

The tribes in this section disposed of their dead by placing the body on a raised platform, and hanging around it the utensils or arms used by the deceased while living.   All these articles were spoiled for earthly use, that they might not tempt the cupidity of any one.   Holes were made in all the kettles and dishes, the bows and arrows were broken, and the skins cut.   They believed that the spirit would need all these things in the other world, and that a spirit touch would make them whole.   They venerated their dead, and their greatest sorrow was to be driven from the spot made sacred by the bones of their forefathers and friends.

If a warrior was killed in battle or in a private feud, his eldest son took it upon himself to avenge his father's death.   If he succeeded, and hung the scalp so taken upon the father's grave, he was entitled to paint a red hand upon his clothing, which was a very high honor.

Generally, marriage among the people of these tribes was an affair of the heart ; although it occasionally happened that a rich suitor, unable to win the maid's affections, but determined to have her, would induce the parents, by valuable presents, to compel her to marry him.   But such cases were not numerous; and the young man had usually to win the girl's affections.   The girls were not allowed to have their grandmothers make proposals to the young men in their behalf, as were the Iroquois

maidens, but relied upon their personal charms to
win a lover; and "the old, old story which is ever
new" was told to them much in the same way as
among the civilized peoples of the world. The
young men wooed very much in the same way as
young men have done and are likely to continue to
do through all time. They made themselves as attractive as possible, took walks by moonlight with
the girl of their choice, and serenaded her on nights
when they could not walk with her. They had a
sort of flute, made from a hollow reed, and upon
this the lover, in the still hours of the night, would
play outside the wigwam of the maiden he loved. If
his suit prospered they would take long daylight
rambles in the grand old native woods, where he
would pour into her willing ear his protestations of
love; tell her of his many exploits in tracking the
wary game, or cause her cheek to blanch with the
story of his more daring and dangerous adventures
upon the war-path. He would fill her trusting soul
with sweet promises of the future, until at last she
yielded the consent he sought. Returning hand in
hand to the village both families would be told of
the engagement, and it would very soon be known
to all the village. On the morrow, if the young
man was unable to make a suitable present to the
girl's parents, he would endeavor to obtain their
consent without the customary gifts. Should he
fail in this, however, he would arrange to steal his
sweetheart; and she, with a charming willingness to
be stolen, would lend him every assistance.

When everything was made ready—and it is
scarcely necessary to say that no time was wasted
in the process—the young man wrapped his buffalo
robe around him, thus concealing his bow and
arrows, tomahawk, and flint knife, and strode away
into the woods as naturally as if nothing was going
to happen. The maiden also, when the way was
clear for her, wrapped herself in *her* buffalo robe,
under which she concealed a kettle and the wooden
dish in which the food was placed, and stole away
to the place agreed upon for meeting her lover.
From there they proceeded to the nearest village in
which the young warrior had relatives, and with
them they remained as husband and wife until they
saw fit to return to their own village. There they
would be received by the parents with open arms;
for it was the custom among these people, where a
couple thus ran away and became husband and wife,
that all opposition to their union should end. In
fact the " stealing " of the bride was little more than
a fiction, the carrying out of which no one made, as
a rule, any serious effort to prevent.

A formal marriage in Indian " high life " was,
however, quite a different affair. After the young
man had wooed and won the maiden of his love, the
engagement was at once announced; and the next
day (for there were no dangerously long engage-
ments) the expectant bridegroom loaded a horse
with presents, and led it in person to the door of
the wigwam of the bride's parents. Here, without
entering or saying a word, he proceeded to unload

the presents, leaving them near the door. If it was near nightfall, or there seemed to be any probability of a storm, the gifts were taken in and cared for. Then a consultation was held among the relatives of the maiden, which etiquette demanded should continue for at least three days, even though the decision was made at once. If this decision were adverse, the young man was informed that he might take away his goods; but if it were favorable, he was advised of the acceptance of his gifts, and a time was fixed when he should receive his bride. When this time arrived, which was usually the same day on which the favorable answer was communicated, the relatives formed a procession headed by the parents of the bride, and she, dressed in her best attire, followed immediately behind them. In silence they marched to within a short distance of the bride-groom's wigwam, and there halted. In a minute or two a warrior, selected by the groom, and whom we might call his " best man," came out to meet them, and placing himself directly in front of the parents, turned his back to them and faced the wigwam of the groom.

Then the parents stepped aside and the bride sprang upon the warrior's back, holding herself there by clinging to his neck; and he, with slow and measured tread, moved toward the wigwam of the groom and upon reaching it the door was promptly thrown open by a relative of the groom. The bride's feet were not permitted to touch the ground until she had crossed the threshold, nor must he who car-

ried her assist her in any manner to hold herself on.
On alighting inside, she rushes to her lover and seats
herself beside him on the bench where he has sat
during the entire time the procession has been
coming, with a countenance as stolid and immovable
as if he had not the slightest interest in the proceed-
ings. Not until the bride had thus seated herself
and placed her hand in that of her lover was the
ceremony complete. As soon as they had joined
hands they became husband and wife, and at once the
tongues of the relatives and friends were unloosed.
The hilarity of the occasion began, and it ended
with a feast prepared by the relatives of the
groom.

The riding of the bride into the groom's wigwam
upon the back of his representative, or best man, was
intended to symbolize the entire dependence of the
wife upon her husband ; that where he goes, she must
go ; that she could do nothing without his consent ;
as, being upon his back, she became a part of him
and subject to his will. Her action in springing
upon his back and clinging there was to show her
entire willingness to become part of him, and that
thenceforth his will should be her will. It was the
Indian way of promising to "love, honor, and obey."

The Indian abounds in superstitions. Had any
unpropitious thing happened—had a white dog
howled or an owl hooted while the wedding procession was marching, the procession would have turned
back to the wigwam of the bride, and the ceremony
would have been delayed until the following day.

Thus we cast a shower of rice or a worn slipper after the departing bride and groom, that they may have happiness and good fortune. Is there so very much difference in the superstitions?

One of the superstitions of the Indians promoted humanity. They had but few cases of idiocy or insanity among them; but they believed that if they injured or maltreated one thus afflicted the Great Spirit would be angry and visit dire calamity upon them. For this reason persons thus afflicted were always very kindly cared for.

This superstition was once of very great service to Professor Hayden, of the United States Geological Survey. One day while engaged in gathering specimens in this section of country, after filling his saddle-bags and pockets with pieces of various kinds of rock, he found he had wandered far from his party, and started to search for them. Seeing some men on horseback, and supposing they were his friends, he rode toward them, but, to his horror, discovered that they were Indians. Knowing that he was in the country of hostiles, he turned his horse and attempted to escape. But his saddle-bags and every pocket were full to overflowing, as was also the tin box containing bugs and insects which hung at his side, and thus handicapped he made but poor headway. The Indians soon overtook him and in sign language ordered him to dismount. They proceeded at once to make an inspection of his possessions. He had nothing with which to defend himself, his outfit being a pocket-knife, hammer, chisel, and watch. These they took, and then began to plunge their hands into his pockets, bringing them out filled with the rock specimens. Again and again they did this, until pockets, pouch, and saddle-bags were all empty ; and as the pile of stones increased upon the ground beside him they burst into loud laughter. Finally they opened the tin box, and when they saw nothing in that but bugs and other insects they quickly closed it, and, looking at each other and then very closely at him, touched their foreheads with the forefinger and made the sign signifying crazy (mind gone). Then they gave back all his things, even picking up the specimens and replacing them carefully in his pockets, pouch, and saddle-bags, and in the sign language told him to mount his horse and go on, which he did with a feeling of thankfulness which can readily be imagined.

Their strongest superstitions were connected with their doctors, or "medicine men," as they called them. They believed them to be supernaturally endowed, and to possess the power of communicating with and exorcising the spirits which caused sickness. They also believed them able to cast a spell over any one at will, thus causing the subject to fall ill or to have bad luck. Great consideration and respect were therefore shown them, not from any love or real regard, but entirely through fear.

Not every one could become a medicine man. In order to reach that distinction the candidate had to be taken in charge by the older medicine men, and pass through a most trying ordeal. He was taken

into the deep forest, and there subjected to a fast
which brought him to the verge of starvation; and
also subjected to self-inflicted cuttings and tortures
of various kinds, to the satisfaction of the old prac-
titioners, until he had dreams of spirits and received
communications from them. If in this preparatory
process he fainted, or if he failed in any respect, he
could never attain the goal of his ambition. What
the spirits communicated to him in dreams he was
required, if possible, to carry out. After passing
successfully through all the minutiæ of this terrible
ordeal, the old medicine men communicated to him
the mysteries of the profession, and he returned to
the village a mere skeleton. But he was then a full-
fledged " medicine man," and as such was allowed to
begin his practice.

Taking advantage of the fear they inspired, the
medicine men were usually great rogues, and made
the most selfish use of their extraordinary opportu-
nities.

When they became ill the Indians ordinarily used
decoctions of various herbs, roots, barks, and berries,
which were prepared and administered by the
women relatives of the sick. The medicine man was
not called until the usual remedies had been tried
and failed to bring relief, and the case came to be
regarded as beyond their control. Then he was sent
for in great haste.

The runner who acted as messenger carried with
him a pipe filled with *Klin-a-can-ic* (the preparation
used as smoking-tobacco), and the fee, which might

consist of a bow and quiver of arrows, a buffalo robe, beaver skins, or any other articles of value in keeping with the financial circumstances of the sick person. On entering the wigwam of the medicine man the runner at once handed him the pipe, which taking, he at once began to smoke. As soon as the pipe was finished the messenger presented the fee and informed the medicine man as to who was in need of his services. If that functionary did not think the fee offered was of sufficient value, he refused to attend the patient until it was made satisfactory; and the runner then returned for more goods. If, however, the fee sent was acceptable, the medicine man at once took his sacred rattle, the only thing needful, and repaired to the wigwam of the sick person.

As this enchanted rattle was the one potent instrument of the medicine man, it is entitled to a description in detail. It was usually about five or six inches in diameter, and was made in various ways. Sometimes it consisted of two pieces of wood hollowed like a gourd, the rattles being placed in the hollow and the pieces fastened together; and sometimes of a turtle shell. But the rattles most esteemed were of raw elk or buffalo hide, wet and stretched over a ball of clay. When the skin had become dry and hard, the clay was dug out at the place where strips of skin had been left for the purpose of fastening upon a handle. Before the handle was attached, the skin, which now firmly retained its ball-shape, was filled with the sacred and enchanted articles to which the virtues of the rattle were attributed. These

articles consisted in part of the finger-bones and
toe-bones of some slain enemy (the more of these, the
more efficacious the rattle); teeth of the beaver and
porcupine; tip-ends of the horns of the buffalo, deer,
and elk; claws and teeth of the bear; shells, agates,
and other stones of various shapes and colors, especially such as had holes through them. This rattle
was priceless; no amount of property would induce
the medicine man to part with it. Hung in his
wigwam, it protected him from all harm, and was
the medium through which he communicated with
friendly spirits, and the charm that kept away all
that were unfriendly.

Armed with this rattle, then, the medicine man
proceeded with slow and solemn tread towards the
wigwam of the patient. Now and again he would
take long strides sidewise and backwards, peering
here and there, making frightful faces, and occasionally making woful howls. Sometimes he wore a
hideous mask and a dress of skins, made to appear
most frightful. This was done in order that, should
any of the spirits afflicting the sick person happen
to be passing that way, they would see what dis-
astrous fate they might expect should they venture
to return; and also (and chiefly) that the people of
the village might be impressed with the mighty
power and importance of the great medicine man.

On entering the wigwam the medicine man
divested himself of his superfluous clothing, took a
seat as far as possible from the patient, and began
shaking his sacred rattle, first faintly, but with rapid-

ly increasing vigor. He also sung his sacred chants, in order to charm the evil spirit that had possession of the patient. He kept this up till he was tired, and then stopped and smoked awhile, returning with renewed energy to his rattling and singing. This was repeated several times, after which, if the sufferer did not feel better, the medicine man tried his more vigorous measures. He rushed at the victim and with violent contortions sucked with his lips the part affected. This operation was sometimes performed with such violence as to draw blood. The medicine man then arose, groaning and writhing and throwing himself into all sorts of postures, as if suffering intense agony. Finally he plunged his head into a bowl of water and was relieved by the passing of the spirit sucked from the sick person into the water. I must not omit to mention that the water had been previously prepared for this purpose by being colored with red clay, in order that the by-standers might not see the spirit as it came from his mouth ; for no human eye could safely look upon it. If the patient did not find himself improved by this proceeding, the medicine man concluded that some animal must have possession of the sick one, and then had recourse to his great and final remedy.

After once more resting and smoking, he procured a piece of bark and marked upon it with red clay a picture of the animal whose spirit was troubling his patient. He next dug a hole in the ground outside the wigwam, filled the hole with water colored with red clay, and immersed the piece of bark therein, and then returned to the wigwam. After many horrible contortions, accompanied with howls and a vigorous shaking of the sacred rattle, he plunged at the patient with a deafening yell, and slapped, pounded, and rubbed him violently from head to foot. During this rather vigorous *massage* treatment he continued his howls, contortions, and grimaces until nearly exhausted; then seizing some part of the patient's body with his teeth, he shook his head like a dog killing a rat, and pretended to tear out a piece of the flesh. This done, he put his hands to the ground and ran " on all fours" out of the wigwam. There he thrust his head into the water in which he had placed the bark, taking care to thoroughly stir up the red clay, so that no one should see the animal's spirit enter the picture he had made of it on the bark. When he arose the bark floated upon the surface of the water, and he ordered some warrior relative of the patient to shoot the spirit, which was done by sending an arrow through the bark. The bark was burned, and the medicine man took his departure.

If the patient recovered, the medicine man received the credit, and was exalted accordingly; if he died, the medicine man admitted that he had made a wrong diagnosis; had failed to hit upon the right animal; that whereas he had taken the spirit possessing the patient to be that of a beaver, it must have been that of a porcupine, and as he did not treat the patient for porcupine, he had died. Was it a vision of the *bacilli* of modern science that the aboriginal medicine man had in his mind?

Usually none but the relatives of the patient are permitted to be present during the visit of the medicine man; but by dint of much persuasion and a present of a five-point blanket to the practitioner, I once obtained the privilege of seeing a man doctored for a severe cold attended with high fever. It was an obstinate case, and all the remedies were employed. The animal in that patient was an otter, and, strange to say, the treatment was efficacious; the patient recovered, and the medicine man often boasted to me afterwards of his wonderful power. He certainly earned his fee, if bodily exertion and fatigue are to be paid for.

But life is not altogether rose-colored, even for the medicine man. It would sometimes happen that he lost more patients than he cured; and then the superstitions of his tribe worked against him. In such cases they thought he had not only lost his power, but that evil spirits had overcome and taken possession of him, and that thereafter his sacred rattle would frighten away the good spirits instead of the evil. When this opinion became prevalent, the medicine man was doomed; for it was then lawful for relatives of any of the patients he had lost to kill him on sight and burn his rattle, and in most cases some of them did it.

Among some tribes the medicine man was the highest power; his word was law. Among others he had the women do the howling and some young man do the rattling or else pound on the tom-tom, contenting himself with merely chanting incantations over the sick.

CHAPTER VI.

THE superstitions of the Indians extended to other matters besides those I have heretofore mentioned. Mr. George Catlin is my authority for the following story of *Wi-jun-jon*, whose portrait he painted.

Wi-jun-jon was the son of the highest chief of the Assiniboins, a brave warrior, young, proud, handsome, and graceful. He had fought many battles; many laurels were his, and he had a just claim to the highest honors his nation could bestow. He was selected by Major Sanford, Indian Agent, to represent his tribe in a delegation which visited the city of Washington in 1832. He had promised his people that he would count all the white men's houses he saw; and in accordance with this promise as he came to them on his journey he began registering their number by cutting a notch on the stem of his pipe for each house. At first the cabins were few and far between and gave him no trouble; but they increased in number as he descended the Missouri River. Soon his pipe stem was covered with notches and he began to notch his war club. This was soon filled also, and when the boat stopped again Wi-jun-jon cut a long

stick, peeled the bark from it, and when the boat
started on its way, began notching the stick. But
this filled up rapidly with notches, and every time
the boat made a landing he would go ashore and get
more sticks, until at length the accumulation of
notched sticks began to trouble him. When at last
the boat arrived at St. Louis, then a town of about
fifteen thousand inhabitants, Wi-jun-jon was completely dumbfounded, and looked upon the great
number of buildings in mute astonishment. After
gazing awhile and evidently realizing the impossibility of keeping up his notch record any longer, he
bundled up his sticks, and with an " Ough!" of disgust pitched them all overboard.

After his visit to Washington, Mr. Catlin accompanied him to his native country. Wi-jun-jon when
he returned to his people was a very different-look-
ing person from the handsome young Indian Wi-jun-
jon as he appeared on setting out to visit the city of
the "Great Father." He had exchanged his beautiful Indian costume for a full-dress military suit
trimmed with gold lace and further adorned with
two immense epaulettes, a shining black stock as
stiff as a board, a pair of high-heeled boots, a bright
red sash, a heavy sword dangling at his side, white
kid gloves upon his hands, and his whole gorgeous
make-up surmounted by a tall beaver hat with a
broad silver-lace band, and a long red feather in its
front. Added to all this magnificence was a blue-cot-
ton umbrella and a large gaudily painted fan. He had
also learned to love the fire-water of the white man.

All this change was brought on Wi-jun-jon by his brief contact with civilization. Of course the metamorphosis in his dress was the work of some white man who desired to possess his handsome Indian costume.

On reaching home in this fantastic garb he was looked at by the people of his tribe in perfect amazement. After the first salutations were over he began telling them of what he had seen. At first they listened respectfully and in wide-eyed wonder; but it was too much for them. They began calling him a liar, and said he had been among the white men, who were all great liars, and had become like them. He sank rapidly into disgrace, and all his prospects of advancement vanished. He was looked upon as a great liar, a character utterly despicable among the Indians. They called him the greatest liar in the nation, and every one shunned and despised him.

After a time he began also to be feared, for they thought he must have received some wonderful power from the Evil Spirit, to be able to invent such stories of novelty and wonder. Their awe, dread, and terror of him became so great that they began to conspire to rid the world of a monster whose superhuman talents must be cut off in order to avert dire calamity to the nation. They held many consultations, for they were at loss to know how they might kill him. Believing that an evil spirit had possessed him, they thought he would be proof against any ordinary arrow, lance, or bullet. Finally

6

one of the young warriors volunteered to undertake his execution. After weeks of hesitation, he had a dream which solved all his difficulties. He dreamed that he must procure by stealth the handle of an old iron pot from the store in the white man's fort, and that that implement would possess the power to overcome the evil spirit. He loitered about the fort for many days, trying to secure the coveted pot-handle. It would not do to ask for it or buy it ; to be efficacious it must be stolen. At last he was successful, and, going into the woods, he spent a whole day straightening and filing the handle so that it would fit into the barrel of his gun. Then with his weapon thus loaded he stealthily approached his victim from behind, placed the muzzle of the gun close to the back of his head, and pulled the trigger. The explosion which followed was like that of a cannon, and it is needless to say that the iron pot-handle overcame the evil spirit, while the recoil nearly killed the gunner as well.

Thus miserably perished poor Wi-jun-jon, a victim to the superstition of his people. Too much knowledge—too high a civilization—had been his undoing. The stories told by him of the sights he had seen were not exaggerations, and it is probable that had he returned to his tribe in his native costume they would in time have come to believe what he said, but the stories *and* the marvellous dress he wore were utterly beyond their acceptance.

The bearing of pain, even when most intense, without making the slightest sign, was one of the proud characteristics of all Indian men. They were taught this from childhood, and some of the tribes had peculiar methods of cultivating stoicism in their children.

A warrior who found a hornets' nest in the woods would inform the villagers. Then all the boys from seven to sixteen years of age would meet and select a leader. Each boy gathered a supply of sticks and stones, and on the next rainy day (hornets are " at home " on rainy days) the boys, divested of all their clothing, even to their moccasins, followed the hunter guide and marched forth to battle with the hornets. Many of the older villagers accompanied them to see the sport, but kept at a respectful distance when the battle began. When they arrived at the spot, the leader placed his young warriors in the most advantageous position for the attack. When all was ready he gave the signal, and the air was soon filled with sticks and stones. It does not take long for hornets to ascertain whence such missiles come, whether thrown by Indians or white boys (as I well know), and they at once began the defence of their castle. The naked bodies of the boys afforded the hornets a fine opportunity for attack, and they improved it with a vigor known only to hornets. It was considered ignominious for any boy to retreat until the nest was entirely demolished. When that had been done the leader gave the signal to his victorious army, and all returned to the village. In case any boy had been stung about the eyes so as to blind him, he was led home by his companions. If a boy cried or showed other sign of pain (and a hornet's sting is much more painful than that of a bee), his companions and the older warriors would cry: "Shame, shame; you are a baby; you are a girl; you will never make a warrior"—which, as we can readily understand, had a powerful influence in making him apparently indifferent to pain. The boys went quickly to their wigwams, where their hurts were dressed by their mothers, and they soon recovered from the effects of the campaign.

Oratory seems to have received less attention among these tribes than among the Iroquois. It is certain that there was little occasion for its practice in their intercourse with the whites, for the latter had become so numerous and powerful by the time they reached this section of the country that scant ceremony was employed in taking the Indians' lands.

There was, however, among the Sioux, a chief named "Two Stars," whose fiery speech is worthy of notice. The occasion was a negotiation of a treaty between his nation and the whites. In opposition to the consummation of this treaty, "Two Stars" addressed his fellow chiefs in the following terms:

"I have lived near the whites and have never been their pensioner. I have suffered from cold in the winter, and never asked clothing; from hunger, and have never asked food. I will live and die on the lands of my forefathers, without asking a favor of an enemy. They call themselves the friends of the Sioux. They are our friends when they want our lands or our furs. They are our worst enemies.

They have trampled us under foot. We do not chase the deer on the prairies as eagerly as they have hunted us down. They steal from us our hunting-grounds, and then win us over by fair words and promises. They furnish us with "fire-water," telling us it is good. They lie. They do this that they may steal our senses and make us fools, so that they may get our lands and furs for nothing. Had not our warriors become women, and learned to fear them, I would gladly raise the war-cry and shout it in their ears. The Great Spirit has indeed forsaken his children, when their warriors and wise men talk of yielding to their foes. I hate them."

One of the tribes inhabiting this section was so unlike all the others, that it seems proper to give some account of the peculiarities of its members. This tribe, known as the Mandans, numbered only about eighteen hundred, and lived in two villages about three miles apart on the bank of the Missouri River. In the matter of complexion as well as in the color and texture of the hair the Mandans were unique among all the Indians of the continent. There is that in their traditions and language which leads to the belief that they were descended from the Welsh voyager, Prince Madoc, and his followers, who sailed from their native country in 1170, and were never afterwards heard from. It is supposed that they sailed up the Mississippi River, and that their vessels becoming disabled or unseaworthy, they intermingled with the natives and finally formed a new tribe.

The evidence in support of this supposition is the

hair and complexion, already spoken of, the frequency of blue eyes among them, and the close resemblance of many words in their language to the Welsh. A list of these words was made by Mr. Catlin, and when compared with words in Welsh having the same meaning the resemblance was so apparent that, as he informs us, " almost any theory would be more credible than that such affinity was the result of accident."

The Mandan villages were strongly fortified, being surrounded from the precipitous bank of the river by a strong stockade of heavy logs, having a deep ditch in front of it. Their houses were partly sunk in the ground, and were built upon strong posts from six to eight feet high, across the tops of which were laid the beams which supported the roof. This roof was covered with clay and soil to such a depth as to shed rain perfectly and also to render the structure absolutely proof against the fire-arrows of an enemy. It was also so strong as to afford a favorite lounging place for the occupants of the dwelling. Mr. Catlin says:

" One is surprised when he enters these houses to see the neatness, comfort, and spacious dimensions of the earth-covered dwellings. They all have a circular form, and are from forty to sixty feet in diameter. An excavation in the centre is used as a fireplace, with a hole in the roof over it for the escape of smoke. The furniture consists of rude bedsteads, with sacking of buffalo skins, and with an ornamental buffalo robe hung in front for a curtain. Between the beds are posts with pegs, upon which the clothing, as well as the arms and accoutrements of the warriors were hung. This arrangement of beds, clothing of different colors, furs and trinkets of various kinds, together with the happy, story-telling groups smoking their pipes, wooing their sweethearts, and embracing their little ones, about the peaceful firesides surrounded with earthen pots and kettles of their own manufacture, presented one of the most picturesque scenes imaginable."

In the centre of each of the villages was a large common in which they exercised and trained their horses, trained and played with their dogs, ran foot-races, and indulged in other out-of-door sports. Their costumes were brilliant and fanciful, ornamented with plumes and colored porcupine quills. Those of the wealthy were exceedingly rich. They were made entirely of skins; a coat of buck-skin, leggins and moccasins of the same, all beautifully fringed and embroidered, and an outer garment of a young buffalo's skin. The head-gear was very elaborate and highly ornamental, being made of ermine skins and the feathers of the war eagle. Some of the chiefs had attained a renown which entitled them to add to their head-dress a pair of buffalo horns, reduced in size and weight, and arranged as they grew upon the animal. The buffalo horns thus worn symbolized courage and power.

Mr. Catlin, who was an artist, wished to paint the portraits of some of their chiefs and warriors. At first he had much difficulty in inducing them to sit for him, as Indians were naturally afraid of new things. Having, however, overcome these fears so far as to get the portrait of one of the chiefs, they were all greatly delighted until they chanced to discover that the eyes of the chief upon the canvas followed them wherever they went. This frightened them exceedingly. They could see it was only a piece of cloth, yet they declared it had life or it could not thus move its eyes. They concluded that some portion of the life of the person represented must have been extracted by the painter, and that consequently the life of that one would be shortened just that much. They also thought that inasmuch as the picture would continue in existence after the death of the original, the quiet of his grave might be disturbed. But the artist finally succeeded in allaying these suspicious fancies, and secured all the sitters he wanted.

The Mandans were cleanly in person, and there were no drunkards or beggars among them. The tribe is now entirely extinct. The smallpox was introduced among them by some white traders, and swept the whole tribe from the face of the earth. Other tribes suffered from the disease at the same time. Major Pilcher, who was then the Indian Superintendent at St. Louis, estimated that no less than twenty-five thousand Indians perished in that section of the country in the course of four or five months. It can readily be imagined that their medicine men would have little power to stay the ravages of such a disease.

This section of country, as well as that to the southward, was inhabited by vast herds of buffalo and wild horses. The Indians tamed great numbers of these horses and became expert horsemen. In order to kill a buffalo with bow and arrows or lance, the hunter had to be within a few feet of him, and as both hands were required to handle the bow, the horses were trained to guide by pressure of the knee or an inclination of the body. They soon became accustomed to this, so that the rider had no difficulty in thus completely commanding their movements.

Buffalo hunting was very exciting, not only on account of the size of the game, but also from the danger involved. The speed of the horse excelled that of the buffalo, but in order to keep his horse fresh the hunter approached the herd as stealthily as possible, and when discovered, dashed after the game at break-neck speed. The buffalo seemed to realize that it was a race for life, and exerted himself to the utmost ; the Indians used only their fleetest and most enduring horses for this work, for the chase was usually a long and trying one. When near enough for the purpose, the hunter aimed an arrow at the heart of his game. The bows used for this purpose were of tremendous power, and such was the force with which the arrow was driven, that, although the full-grown buffalo is as large as the tame ox, the arrow frequently passed completely through the body.

But the buffalo, sometimes before and sometimes after being wounded, would turn with the quickness of thought upon the hunter and try to impale him with his horns. Against such an attack the hunter had to trust entirely to the sagacity and swift movements of his horse. The quickness with which the horse would discern the slightest motion on the part of the buffalo to turn upon his pursuer was wonderful. Although going at full speed, he would always be ready to dodge. The hunter must be very expert and agile to avoid being thrown by a sudden and unexpected side-spring of his horse; for if unhorsed he would be gored and trampled to death in a moment by the infuriated buffalo. The Indians sometimes covered themselves with wolf skins and crept within shooting distance of the buffalo on their hands and knees.

The catching of wild horses furnished these Indians with fine sport. They used a lasso, or lariat, about fifty feet long, sometimes made of hair, but usually of braided rawhide, rubbed until it was as soft and pliable as rope. This they could throw with great precision.

The men and boys, and sometimes the more courageous of the girls, had great sport breaking in these wild horses to ride. They fastened a rope made of rawhide around the lower jaw of the horse with a " clove hitch," and then blindfolded him. They next fastened another rope around his body, leaving it just loose enough for the rider to put his knees under it. It is a singular fact that a wild horse would not stir while he was blindfolded. When the rider was mounted and ready, the blind was removed; the rider applied the whip or quirt, and away went the frightened horse, **bounding** over the prairie like a startled deer. The rider could **not** be **thrown,** because the rope over his **knees held** him fast, yet, if the horse should fall, he could easily free himself. The horse was guided by striking him on either side of the head with the whip, and when he was nearly exhausted his rider would make him **return to the** starting-point. After a few such experiences the horse would be thoroughly broken.

It sometimes happened that when the rider was mounted and the blind removed, the horse, instead of starting off on a run, would stand and jump, coming down with his legs as stiff as rails. This was called " bucking," and was great sport for the spectators, but not for the unfortunate rider. The terrible jolting soon gave him such a pain in the side that he was glad to jump or roll off, and his evolutions in the air and scrambling on the ground to get out of the way of the horse afforded much amusement to his companions.

The Comanche was a daring horseman. In battle he would hang at the side of his horse leaving nothing except his foot visible on the other side, and at the same time fire his arrows at the foe from under his horse's neck while running at full speed. He was enabled to do this by having a short piece of lasso passed around the neck of his horse and each end firmly braided into the mane at the withers, thus forming a loop into which he could slip his elbow to sustain the weight of his body while balancing

himself by means of one foot thrown over the horse's
back.   This also enabled him at any time to regain
his position.   By the use of these tactics he was protected by the body of his horse from the arrows of
the foe.   In order to kill him the enemy must first
disable his horse, and while they were doing that
the Comanche could get in a good deal of bloody
work.

The Comanches had a different method from that
already described for breaking in the wild horses.
Having caught one with the lasso, they drew the
noose tight around the captive's throat, choking him
until he fell.   Then dismounting, they blindfolded
him and tied his front feet together.   After doing
this they patted him and handled him all over,
breathed in his nostrils, and worked kindly with him
until the horse became accustomed to the treatment ; and, strange as it may seem, in an hour or
two they would loosen his feet, and one of the party
would mount and ride him home.

CHAPTER VII.

THAT portion of North America west of the Rocky Mountains and north of the thirty-third parallel was also inhabited by numerous tribes or nations of Indians, alike in general aspect, but differing widely in certain particulars.

Those in the extreme north were called Esquimo. Indeed, this same race, each tribe varying but little from the others, occupied the entire northern portion of the continent, from Greenland to Behring Sea. They were short of stature, slovenly, and untidy. Not so warlike as the Indians to the south of them, they were very suspicious of strangers, but kind and hospitable after becoming acquainted. Brownell says: "The Esquimo received little better treatment at the hands of the early European discoverers than did their brethren farther south. It is strange to read of the coolness with which those adventurers speak of the emormities not unfrequently committed against the unoffending and ignorant natives. The meeting of several 'wild men' (as the adventurers called them) and the killing of one of them to make the rest tractable, is mentioned as a passing and ordinary event."

The dwellings of the Esquimo were of two kinds. Those used in summer were movable, and built of poles and skins, similar to those of the southern Indians; while their winter habitations were constructed of blocks of ice, cut and shaped with astonishing precision. They were familiar with the principle of the arch, and made use of it with the key-stone shaped in blocks of ice. These dwellings were almost hermetically tight, as all the interstices between the layers of ice, and the small holes here and there, were filled with snow, and water was dashed upon these until the whole became one mass of solid ice. They were thus made quite warm, and but for the filthy habits of the people, they would have been comfortable, notwithstanding the intensely cold weather. Thin, and nearly transparent cakes of ice were inserted here and there in the roof for the admission of light. The Esquimo lived on oil and blubber obtained from the whale, walrus, and seal, together with the meat of the reindeer, musk-ox, and water-fowl, besides fish. The only vegetable foods they had were a species of willow which they ground in a mortar, the leaves of the sorrel, a few berries, and some roots which they also pounded up. The lean meat of the whale, seal, and such other as they obtained, was dried, smoked, and pounded up with some fat into a dry mixture called "pemmican," which would keep for use during their long, dark winter.

They built large canoes in which to carry the family and goods, and exhibited great dexterity in the manufacture and management of the style of canoe called by them "kaiak." This would carry but one person. It was a light, frail structure, having small pieces of wood for the frame, and covered top and bottom, with small seal-skins so neatly and strongly sewed together as to be perfectly watertight above and below. The structure was usually twenty to twenty-five feet long, two feet wide, and about a foot deep. In the centre a hole was cut through the skin just large enough for a man to get in and have his body completely fill it. He used a paddle with a blade at each end. In this frail craft the Esquimo would go long distances out to sea and attack the seal with a harpoon having a buoy of sealskin fastened to the end of the line to prevent the seal from sinking when killed. In case of a capsize, which seldom happened, the boatman could easily right himself with his paddle. The kaiak was a safe boat with an Esquimo, but woe to any white man who attempted its use.

The Esquimo used dogs as their beasts of burden, and did all travelling with them after the water had frozen so that they could not go in boats. The runners of their sleds were made of pieces of wood, or sometimes of the jawbones of the whale, fastened together at a distance of about two feet apart, with cross-pieces and thongs upon which a skin was stretched and the load deposited. The dogs were attached to separate tethers of different lengths, the leader being sometimes as far as twenty feet from the sledge. How they managed to drive them in this way without getting them entangled is a mystery to white men. They used a whip with a short stock and a lash long enough to reach the leader, and would make sixty miles a day with a load averaging one hundred pounds for each dog. They made the sledge run easy by turning it up and pouring water upon the runners and letting it freeze, thus forming shoes of ice. Great distances were often travelled over the frozen waters, and great loads transported. Snow-shoes were also used to some extent in travelling.

The clothing of the Esquimo consisted wholly of furs. The inner garments were worn with the fur next the body, and the outer garments with fur outside. These garments were neatly and strongly sewn together, and made quite ornamental by tastefully mixing different colored furs; teeth of animals were hung in the borders, and foxes' noses sewed on like buttons. They all wore high waterproof boots made of sealskin. The women wore the same kind of underclothing as the men, while their outer dress consisted of a moderately close-fitting waist or jacket, together with a short skirt and trousers. They practised tattooing, which was done by drawing a thread saturated with oil and soot under the skin.

The only fires used by the Esquimo for warmth or cooking were made by suspending a piece of blubber over a shallow stone dish, around the edge of which twisted moss was so placed as to form a wick. The heat extracted the oil from the blubber, and as it dripped into the dish a continual supply of fuel was kept up. They kept the temperature of their houses a little below freezing, for if it rose higher the roof would be melted. Always accustomed to this temperature indoors, they could endure intense cold while moving about outside. Their weapons were bows and arrows, lances, and harpoons, all of which were quite ingeniously made. As regards religion, Mr. Parry says: "They do not appear to have any idea of the existence of one Supreme Being, nor, indeed, can they be said to entertain any notions on this subject which may be dignified with the name of religion." They had quite a number of dances; and they were not warlike, but quite domestic in their habits and tastes, very contented, and, in their way, happy.

In complexion the Esquimo are fair, almost white. They are of medium stature, good proportion, muscular, and active, while their feet and hands were small and of fine shape. They seldom mingled or associated with any of the tribes to the south, and therefore have remained almost without change from generation to generation. They differed from the Esquimo upon the eastern coast in disposition and in their treatment of children. This was perhaps due to the fact that they had not so severe a struggle for existence as did their eastern brethren, and hence had more time for leisure and amusement. They had three months of winter, during which time they did not see the sun; three months of continuous day during which the sun never set; and three months of twilight at the end of these seasons.

7

They displayed considerable ingenuity in catching game. For taking the reindeer they made corrals of turf, rubbish, or drift-wood, and also made piles of turf to represent men, standing them a short distance apart in two rows diverging from the mouth of the corral, sometimes to the distance of two miles. They then drove the deer into the broad opening between these two rows, and followed them up to the corral. The deer, taking the piles of turf for men, would not attempt to pass out between them, and were thus driven into the corral, where it was impossible for them to escape the arrows of the hunters.

But their manner of hunting and killing the polar bear was unique. Knowing the bear to be fond of blubber, they took a piece of it as large as a man's fist, and after letting it freeze hollowed out the centre sufficiently to admit a strip of whalebone coiled into a spring. This was covered with more blubber and the whole again frozen. Dressing themselves to look like seals (the bear's favorite food) the hunters took several of these frozen balls and started out. When a bear was discovered they approached near enough for him to see them. As he began to creep stealthily toward them they slowly retreated, dropping a number of the balls in such a way that the bear in following them must surely come upon the balls. Bruin seeing these delicate morsels swallowed them whole and continued his stealthy chase of the supposed seals. But he did not progress far before the blubber melted and released the whalebone springs. These new " works " in his internal economy soon put him in such agony that he rolled and tumbled upon the ice, and became an easy victim to the weapons of the hunters.

The young Esquimo who desired to marry had first to obtain the consent of the mother of the girl he wished to woo, after which he was at liberty to present her with furs for a suit of clothes. If she accepted the gift the act constituted a formal engagement ; and when she made up the furs and put them on she became, without further ceremony or formality, his wife.

The Koniagas lived to the southward of the Esquimo. They were much larger in stature than the Esquimo, and their skin was much whiter than that of the Indians farther south. They were also well formed, and would have been fine-looking but for the horrible fashion they had of deforming their ears, nose, and under lip with what they considered ornaments.

The dress of the poorer class among the Koniagas was made of skins somewhat after the manner of the Esquimo ; but some who were in better circumstances wore a garment called a " parka." This was a cloak, made of bird skins neatly sewed together. It required as many as a hundred skins to make a parka. As needles they used certain bones from fish, and it was surprising to see what fine work they did with only bits of sinew for thread. The parka was fringed and ornamented at top and bottom, but the elaborate work was upon the girdle about the waist. This was beautifully embroidered. Only the

rich could afford this kind of garment. If caught
out in bad weather in this their gala dress they protected the feathers with a waterproof cloak made
from the intestines of the walrus and seal, tanned,
rubbed pliable, and sewed together so neatly as to
be impervious to water, even at the seams. They
also made high boots of the skin from the neck of
the seal, and soled them with the thick skin of the
whale. These boots were also waterproof and very
strong.

They had no marriage ceremony. Marriage was a
simple agreement between the parties, and as soon
as it was approved by the father of the maiden the
lovers became husband and wife.

The Aleuts inhabited the Aleutian Archipelago,
and numbered twenty-two different clans, or divisions, nearly every island having its own clan. Our
earliest knowledge of them comes from the Russian
explorer, Novodsikoff, who visited the archipelago
in 1745. As soon as he returned to his native land
and published the story of the wonderful number
and variety of fur-bearing animals he found there,
the waters in that region became alive with Russian
adventurers. They swarmed upon the islands, laid
tribute upon the Indians, and treated them so cruelly
and wickedly that their numbers were quickly
reduced from ten thousand to barely a thousand.

In appearance the Aleuts resembled the Koniagas.
Their features were strongly marked, and those who
saw them as they originally appeared were impressed
with the intelligent and benevolent expression of

their faces. A missionary who lived ten years among them says that during all that time there was not a single fight among the natives. This is evidence of the quiet and peaceful disposition which rendered them an easy prey to the Russian invaders. Their dress was similar to that of the Koniagas, with the addition of a high peaked hat, made of wood or leather. This hat had a long brim in front to protect the eyes of the wearer from the glare of the sun upon the water and snow, and was ornamented at the back by hanging upon it the beards of sea-lions. The front was usually carved to represent some animal. They lived during the long winter in permanent houses, but in the summer a canoe turned bottom upward formed their only shelter. They built their canoes of skins in the same way as the Esquimo. Good planks and boards were made by them by splitting cedar logs and working the slabs down straight and smooth with the aid of fire, stone axes, and stone scrapers.

They made much use of this kind of lumber in building their winter houses, and in constructing traps for bears. To make a bear-trap they took a plank about two feet square and drove firmly into it many sharp bones, upon the projecting ends of which a barb had been cut. They then buried the plank thus prepared under leaves and other light rubbish in the track of the bear. When the unsuspecting animal stepped upon it, his great weight drove the barbed bones deep into his foot ; the pain at once caused him to use the other foot to relieve

the first, and that soon became fastened also.   Next
the hind feet came to relieve those already impris-
oned, and it was not long until he was a prisoner
with all four feet pinned to the plank, and an easy
prey to the hunters who had been watching the
trap.

The Aleuts had some religious ceremonies, the
women taking the most active part in them.   In the
winter they were accustomed to amuse themselves
by a variety of games.   Among these, one of the
greatest favorites was an imitation of the chase, in
which one party of young men and maidens acted
the part of hunters, and another party that of game.

By some historians the Esquimo, Koniagas, and
Aleuts are all called Esquimo.   I do not, however,
concur in so classing them.   It is true that there are
many points of resemblance ; but they differed very
materially in stature, in features, and in language ;
many of their customs were different ; they did not
associate or intermarry with each other ; and they
were occasionally at war.

The next large family, or tribe, to the southward
were the Thlinkeets ; and whatever may be the prevailing opinion in regard to the three tribes just
mentioned, the Thlinkeets were so different from
any of the three that they cannot with any propriety
be classed as Esquimo.

The Thlinkeets inhabited a vast territory of which
the climate as a whole was temperate, or not subject
to any great extremes either of heat or cold.   These
conditions led to more extended wanderings and a

greater amount of physical exercise, and tended to expand the mind and develop the body. The skin of the Thlinkeets was much whiter than that of the Indians who lived farther south ; and if they had not distorted their features by piercing their ears, nose, and lips, and filling them with bones and shells, they would have been quite comely, for nature had done much to make them so. But this hideousness was called beautiful by them ; and the Thlinkeet girl who aspired to be a belle must wear as many of these "decorations" as possible, and the larger the lip ornament the more beautiful she was esteemed. Slave women and their children were not allowed the privilege of having their ears, nose, or lips pierced, and some of them were really handsome.

The Thlinkeets made their canoes of wood, usually of the white cedar, which grows plentifully and of large size all over the northwestern portion of the continent. They were skilled in the manufacture of war implements, bows and arrows, lances, shields, flint knives, etc. Their arrows and lances were tipped with flint, or, sometimes with copper, as that metal was found in their country and they knew how to work it to some extent. In case a point was lost from an arrow or a lance, and they had not the opportunity to replace it, they would harden the end by putting it into the fire, and then scrape it to a point. They also showed much ingenuity in the manufacture of domestic implements from stone, wood, and grasses. They made baskets so thick and closely plaited that they would hold water. In such a basket they cooked their food, making the water boil by putting in heated stones. From black slate they made bowls, pipes, and other utensils. The carving on their pipes was unique and beautiful. I have seen some of these as much as fifteen or eighteen inches in length, three or four inches broad, and three quarters of an inch in thickness, which were one continuous mass of carvings of animals, birds, and men, the whole held together by the ingenious intertwining of the arms, legs, and bodies of the different figures. Frequently the heads of the men and animals were carved in ivory and cemented into the neck of the stone figure cut in the pipe.

Their marriage was by agreement, and presents were exchanged. The ceremony consisted of a general assembling of the friends of the contracting parties at a grand feast. Presents were distributed, and when the feast was over the bride and groom joined hands and seated themselves upon one bench. They were then married ; but this was only the beginning of their troubles. Custom required them to fast two days ; then, after taking a little food, to fast two days more, after which they associated together only in the same way as they had done prior to their marriage. This they were obliged to endure for four weeks, at the end of which they could begin living together as husband and wife.

The Thlinkeets were fond of music, and indulged in much dancing in the winter. They burned their dead, placing their ashes in a box on platforms elevated upon poles. They also showed them great reverence, and made grand feasts a part of the funeral ceremony. They were cruel to prisoners and slaves, and were inveterate gamblers; but they were brave, intelligent, and industrious, and very respectful to the aged and to women.

CHAPTER VIII.

THE Tinneh family comprised thirty-four different tribes, some large and powerful, and some small. They inhabited a large section of the country to the eastward of that occupied by the tribes last mentioned. Their lands did not reach the Arctic Ocean, and barely touched the Pacific at Cook's Inlet. They differed but slightly from the Thlinkeets.

Among the tribes of the Tinneh family marriages were unaccompanied by any ceremony, and were made either by agreement between the parties or by purchase of the maiden. If made by purchase, the girl had nothing whatever to say about the matter, but must go with the purchaser, no matter what her feelings toward him might be. Many a Tinneh girl has taken her own life rather than become a wife to the man who bought her.

These tribes had all their dances at night as there prevailed among them a strong superstition against dancing in the sunlight. They were an indolent people, but hospitable and amusement-loving. The finger nails of their female children were never cut until they had reached the age of four years, lest they should grow up to be lazy women. Lazy women were not tolerated in Indian society. The case was somewhat different with the men.

The " hiaqua "—a shell shaped like an elephant's tusk, but only about one eighth of an inch in thickness at the base, and from one to two and a half inches long—constituted their currency, as it did also that of the Indians of the coast. Every one obtained as many as possible of these shells the same as white people accumulate dollars. One hundred and fifty to two hundred hiaquas would buy as fine a girl as there was in the tribe for a wife ; from fifty to seventy-five would buy a female slave, and an addition of twenty-five hiaquas would make a sum sufficient to buy a man slave.

A person who had killed another, either by accident or design, was safe from the vengeance of the relatives of the murdered one if he could get into the wigwam of a chief, provided the chief would allow him to remain there ; and if he was permitted to wear some part of the chief's clothing, he was safe so long as he had that on, regardless of where he was. This gave him time usually to negotiate with the relatives of the person he had killed, and, by a payment of goods or hiaquas, to save himself harmless. This custom had a great tendency to strengthen the power of the chief ; as every one desired to have his good-will, so that should he or one of his relatives under any circumstances kill any person, the chief, recognizing his friendship, would not turn him from the asylum of his wigwam, should he flee to it for protection.

The Tinneh tribes, like the Thlinkeets, were inveterate gamblers, frequently staking all they possessed—even their wives. Their principal game was played with marked beaver teeth. These were thrown into the air, and those that fell with the marks up counted. They had other games for gambling, one of which was hiding sticks.

Among these tribes, if the medicine man did not heal the sick one, he was obliged to return the fee which had been paid him. Slavery existed in its worst forms. Upon the death of a slave-owner, one or more of his slaves were killed to accompany him and wait upon him in the spirit land. In the case of a chief, two at least were sacrificed.

They burned their dead, and, strangely, they had a custom similar to that which formerly prevailed in India in regard to the widow. She was compelled to mount the burning pile upon which lay her husband's body and throw herself upon him; but she was allowed to escape after her hair had been burned off. After escaping from the funeral pyre she was obliged, regardless of pain, to tend and keep it burning. After the body was consumed the ashes were gathered and placed in a bag which was carried constantly by the widow for two years. During all this time she must dress in rags and mourn her loss. When the period of her mourning had expired, the bag of ashes was buried, the people of her village made a feast for her, and thenceforth she was free to marry again if she desired.

These Indians possessed many good qualities.

They were brave, frank, and candid, and were also strong and fine-looking. Considerable attention was given by them to personal cleanliness. Most of the men were above six feet in height, and the women were comely. The Chinese custom of bandaging the feet of the female infants to make them small prevailed among them to some extent. The women outlived the men by an average of fifteen years. They made pottery from clay, moulding it by hand, drying it in the sun, and afterwards baking it in the fire. They made a good quality of glue from the feet of the elk and deer. Their canoes were made of strips of bark sewed together with fine roots pounded to fibre, and the seams were made tight by means of pitch from fir and spruce trees.

The men of these tribes, by means of their size and strength, were famous warriors. In long marches and hand-to-hand contests these qualities were of great advantage to them. Like most Indians, they had three general reasons for going to war; first, revenge for some real or fancied injury; second, avarice, which impelled them to capture slaves to use or sell; and, third, to weaken their enemies by destroying their resources. This last was their reason for killing the women and children of their foemen, when they could not make them prisoners; for, they argued, the women, if left alive, would bear children, and the male children would eventually become warriors, whom they would some time have to fight. We must admit the soundness of their logic, however much we may question the system of ethics on which it was based.

Returning to the coast, the next nation of note south of the Thlinkeets was that of the Haidahs, whose principal tribes inhabited Queen Charlotte's Island and the adjacent coast of the mainland. They numbered some thirty different tribes in their family, and occupied a country about three hundred miles long by one hundred miles wide. Their country was divided from that of the eastern Indians by the Cascade Mountains, which range extends north and south through British America, down to and into California, at a distance of one hundred to one hundred and fifty miles from the Pacific Ocean. The climate differed materially on the east and west sides of this mountain range, and this fact had a marked effect upon the Indians inhabiting the two sections. On the west, from the foothills to the coast, the temperature, owing to the warm currents of the ocean, never reached extremes of either heat or cold. In this equable climate there was little to incite the people to any great exertion. Hence it was that, although the country was finely wooded and abounded in game, the Haidahs hunted but little— just enough to furnish skins for clothing and bedding. Fish were abundant in the ocean and the rivers, and as it was quite in accord with the indolent habits of these people to subsist on that which was obtained with least exertion, their food consisted principally of fish, berries, and roots. The women and female slaves gathered and dried the berries for winter use, while the men and male slaves caught the fish and turned them over to the women to be cared for. The heads and tails of the salmon and halibut were cut off and eaten during the summer, while their bodies were split in two and hung up in the sun and smoked to cure for winter use. They knew nothing of salt until the whites came, and even then preferred fish dried without it. The climate was so mild that they did not need to feed their bodily furnaces with the fat of blubber, as did the Esquimo ; so this was only used for fire and light.

They hunted the whale, because its blubber, oil, and bone were available in traffic with their northern neighbors. With these they could purchase slaves and skins. They were the most expert whale fishers upon the coast. This showed them to be as courageous and enterprising as the inland tribes who lived by hunting ; for it required no less skill and daring to capture the whale in his native element than to kill the bear, panther, and elk in the forest. Both occupations seemed to have an elevating effect upon the faculties of the Indians who pursued them ; for they were certainly superior, mentally as well as physically, to those Indians who lived solely by fishing in inland waters.

The Haidahs were tall and well formed, the peers in personal appearance of any Indians on the coast. They were quite light of complexion, some of them being almost as fair as Europeans, with hair of a light brown instead of the usual black of other tribes. They frequently wore the hair short, to save the labor of taking care of it. Poole says of them that "some of the women have exceedingly handsome

faces and symmetrical figures," and that he was
"impressed by the manly beauty and bodily proportions of the Queen Charlotte Islanders." Vancouver
says: "The prominence of their countenances and
the regularity of their features resembled the northern Europeans." Dunn says that he saw "a chief
of gigantic proportions, stately air, manly bearing,
and all the external characteristics of dignity, with a
symmetrical figure and a perfect order of European
contour." I have seen some of these Indians whose
race would not be suspected in a company of whites
by reason of any difference in color or in contour of
features, and whom it would require close inspection
to recognize as Indians, if dressed in the garb of the
white man.

Some of their houses were built on the tops of
posts, twenty-five or thirty feet high. Access was
gained to such houses by means of a ladder formed
of a log or small tree, in which deep notches were
cut. The posts were often carved to represent grotesque human figures, beasts, or birds. Such posts
have been mistaken for idols by early discoverers,
but it is now certain that no form of idolatry ever
existed among these Indians. Vancouver saw one
of their houses that was built on a platform thirty
feet from the ground. The house was forty-five feet
wide and one hundred and five feet long, with a
nearly flat roof raised ten or twelve feet above the
platform. This was made of planks split from cedar
trees. They did not, however, build all their houses
in the air. Many of them were much smaller, and

built on the ground. This was the method of building in many of their villages, when the dwellings stood in rows similar to those in a city street. They had also other styles of architecture. Poole mentions a house fifty feet square and fifty in height, ten feet of which was under ground. The houses built upon elevated platforms were supposed to be for refuge in case of an attack.

The weapons of the Haidahs were well made, and were of much the same style as those of others that have been described. The harpoon with which they captured the whale or seal was ingeniously contrived. A thong was tied around the centre of the barb and extended to the handle, some four or five feet from its lower end ; and when the point had penetrated the skin of the animal, a sharp pull on the thong served to turn the barb sidewise in the flesh, and prevented its tearing out. The spears used for taking salmon and halibut were much smaller, but supplied with the same device. These people had at the time the whites first came among them a few harpoons, spears, and arrow-heads tipped with iron, and it has been a matter of much speculation where they obtained the metal for this purpose. The oldest men among them could not tell where it came from ; but simply said they had always had it. It is supposed that it came from Russia or from wrecks along the coast. The Haidahs made bows from the wood of the yew tree, gluing strips of sinew over the back to give additional strength and elasticity. I have in my possession one of these bows with which I have seen an Indian throw an arrow nearly a thousand feet. They made strong serviceable fishing-nets from wild hemp and the fibre of cedar bark. Their household utensils, which were quite numerous, were made of wood, bone, stone, and horn. Like the Thlinkeets, they carved beautiful pipes from stone and ivory, excelling in this art all other tribes. They used both ivory and pearl for inlaying these pipes.

The thing for which these Indians were most noted however, was the size and beauty of their canoes. It was really surprising to see what they could do in this line, with their rude tools. Having selected such a tree as they wanted to use for the canoe, they felled it by burning, and cut off the trunk to the proper length, again utilizing fire for the purpose. If the canoe was to be a comparatively small one, they would, before proceeding further, split the log through the centre, using wooden or elk-horn wedges for the purpose. But if they were building a large canoe, they would, without splitting the log, build fires in several places on the upper side of it as it lay on the ground, allowing the burning to go on until enough of the wood was charred to begin the process of cutting out with stone axes, chisels, and scrapers. This burning, digging, and scraping was continued, both inside and out, until the canoe was fashioned to their liking. The skill and ingenuity displayed in the whole process was remarkable. Not only would the canoe be most graceful in shape, but of a perfectly even thickness, not exceeding one inch at the sides and two inches at the bottom, and the whole so nicely balanced that it would of itself ride the water on a perfectly even keel. In the case of extra large canoes, the prow and stern were made of separate pieces, extending much above the sides and strongly fastened with dowel pins and bark or sinew lacings. Usually the prow and stern were artistically carved, after some animal, fish, or bird, the prow representing the head and the stern the tail. These carvings were sometimes very elaborate, especially on the largest war canoes, and when painted in their fantastic style presented an appearance both formidable and grotesque. They were propelled with single-bladed paddles, each oarsman having one. They had canoes from a size only sufficient to carry one man, up to a size that would carry seventy-five to a hundred. I once counted sixty-eight men and several women and children in one of their larger canoes, and there was not the slightest suggestion of its being overloaded. They did not hesitate at all about going out upon the ocean in these boats, and they navigated the coast for long distances. They had no knowledge of sails and their use, until taught by the whites.

In the matter of musical instruments they had a drum similar to that used by other Indians; a tambourine, made by stretching a wet skin over hoops of different sizes and thus letting it dry; and a flute made from slate stone. They drilled a hole through the entire length of the stone, by means of a piece of sharp flint secured to the end of a reed or rounded stick. The slate used by them was quite soft when first taken from its bed, and yielded easily to the drill. Poole says he " saw a flute, two of the keys representing frogs in a sitting posture, the carving of which would have done credit to an European modeller." Simpson says that he found " very accurate charts of the adjacent Pacific coasts made by this tribe." Hale says they had " very fine cups, plates, pipes, little images, and various ornaments, wrought with surprising elegance and taste." This artistic skill and knowledge of practical drawing show that these people were capable of making very material advances in civilization.

There was in their country a peculiar breed of white dogs with very long hair. These dogs the Indians sheared each year, like sheep, and the hair thus obtained, when mixed with the fibre of wild hemp and cedar roots, was woven into blankets and robes of very good quality. The fibre spoken of was made by first boiling the hemp or cedar roots and then pounding between flat stones. The woody part thus separated, was carefully picked out, after which the fibre was twisted into fine or coarse threads as desired. Their method of weaving closely resembled that of the old Egyptians.

Among the Haidahs the chieftaincies were, as in many other tribes, mostly hereditary ; from which it sometimes happened that a woman became a chief.

A superstition prevailed among them that all well-starred marriages must be celebrated upon the water. After gifts are presented and accepted, as among other tribes, the friends build a platform on canoes at a moderate distance from the shore. After the completion of this work the bride and her friends, dressed in their best attire, proceed in canoes to the floating platform ; while the groom and his friends, also dressed in gala attire, approach it from an opposite direction. Meeting upon the platform, more presents are given, and the groom passes from his side of the platform to the side of the bride, takes her hand, and leads her over to his side. Then follows a dance in which all but the bride and groom take part ; and while this is progressing the groom places his bride in his own canoe, and paddling to the shore, takes her to his wigwam. The dancing ended, the bride's party return to the land, putting the presents in the place occupied by the bride on the outward trip.

The Haidahs, like all Indians, were great gamblers. Their principal game was a very simple one of " odd and even." Each player had from forty to fifty round sticks, and each in turn would hide as many as he chose under a mat or blanket, the others simply guessing "odd " or "even." It was purely a game of chance. He who guessed right took as many sticks as were hidden ; if he guessed wrong he was obliged to give his opponent the same number. The game was ended when one had won all his adversary's sticks. They would sometimes stake all they had in the world on this simple game. They had no intoxicating drinks prior to the coming of the whites, and personal quarrels between members of the same tribe were almost unknown.

The next nation to the southward was that of the
Nootkas. This family was composed of thirty-seven
tribes. They were somewhat smaller than the Haidahs, and a shade darker. They all wore their hair
long, and it was a disgrace for a man or woman to
have short hair—the mark of a slave. The women
took great care of their hair, braiding it neatly,
arranging it in many curious ways, and decorating it
with shells and various ivory ornaments.

The singular custom of flattening the head obtained
among these Indians, though not to the same extent
as with the Chinooks, of whom an account will be
given in the next chapter. When the child was four
days old it was bound upon the pappoose-board (identical in style with that of the Iroquois, heretofore
described), and underwent the flattening process. In
a few months the head of the child would not be
more than two inches thick from front to back at
the crown, but would be spread sidewise to a great
extent. As the child grew older, the head would
resume something of its natural shape, and by the
time it was full grown, the head was much more
rounded; but the effect of the flattening process
always remained unmistakably visible. This custom
was not universal among the Nootkas; but, unques-
tionable deformity as it was, it was among them a
mark of nobility. No person born a slave ever had
the honor of having the head flattened.

In warm weather these Indians dressed chiefly in
paint, the men much more elaborately than the
women. After the age of twenty-five the women

ceased to adorn themselves with paint. They no longer considered themselves young, and therefore yielded the palm of beauty to the more youthful maidens. In cold weather the dress was a square blanket, with a hole in the middle, through which the head of the wearer was thrust. The garment thus rested upon the shoulders, and was sometimes held in at the waist by a belt. The blankets of the rich were bordered with fine fur, and quite richly decorated, but those of the poor were of coarse material, without any decoration. The head was usually left uncovered.

The principal sustenance of the Nootkas was fish, which they caught with net, spear, and hook. They had an ingenious plan of covering the bottom of the streams in certain places with white stones, so that they could more clearly see and readily spear the fish as they crossed. They used wooden canoes, similar to those of the Haidahs, but were not so skilful in building them. Slavery obtained among them, and the slave-trade formed the principal part of their dealings with other tribes. War and stealing, or kidnapping, were the principal sources of supply.

The amusement of the Nootkas consisted mainly of feasting, dancing, and gambling. They had athletic games, among which were hooking their little fingers together and pulling, as a test of strength, jumping, wrestling, running and swimming races on a wager. They were strong believers in dreams, witchcraft, and evil spirits; and through this belief their medicine men, who practised all

kinds of sorcery, obtained great power. They claimed
that all sickness was caused by the anger of the evil
spirits, and their treatment was directed to appeasing
such spirits. Very poor persons and slaves were
allowed to die quietly, as they had nothing with
which to pay a fee to the doctor.

This tribe had some superstitions similar to those
which have found a place among white races in different ages of the world. One of these was that
love could be incited by certain potions or powders.
A love-lorn Nootka maiden would seek an opportunity to stealthily sprinkle her love powder into the
food of the young brave of her choice, and if successful was very happy, and would spend much of the
day in dressing her luxuriant hair and adorning herself with paint. When the sun went down and the
soft, cool evening came, she stationed herself where
she thought her wished-for lover would see her, and,
—singing low and sweet her song of love, awaited his
coming. If she was fortunate, and he made his appearance, her happiness was complete. If he failed
to come that way, she thought some evil spirit had
overcome her love-potion, and as its spell lasted but
one day she would have to try again.

Still journeying southward, we come to Puget
Sound, an inlet of the ocean many miles in extent,
quite broad, and filled with islands and long prom-
ontories. Around this sound were many tribes of
Indians, but they differed so slightly from the Nootkas that I shall have but little to say about them.

They made use of the torch to catch game—a device entirely unknown among the more northern Indians. They hunted elk and deer at night, attracting them within bow-shot by the bright lights. At certain points on the coast where great flocks of water-fowl flew from point to point, they erected tall poles and on them stretched nets made of cords manufactured from wild hemp and cedar roots. Getting behind these at night, they would raise their torches, and it was astonishing to see what numbers of birds would fly against the nets and drop to the ground, stunned by the force of the collision and thus rendered powerless to escape the hunters. In all other matters these tribes so closely resembled the Nootkas that no further description of them is necessary.

CHAPTER IX.

WHEN, upwards of forty years ago, I first became acquainted with the Indians inhabiting California and Oregon, they were all much alike and no one tribe was dominant. There were many large and some small tribes having their homes in the country west of the Rocky and Sierra Nevada Mountains and north of the thirty-third parallel of north latitude. Inasmuch, however, as their habits and customs did not vary sufficiently among themselves or from other Indians to make a separate account necessary, I shall confine myself to a description of the Chinooks, upon the Columbia River, in Oregon, as a representative tribe of this whole section.

The Chinooks then occupied the banks of the Columbia near its mouth, and were probably the best representatives of the Indians inhabiting the section of country mentioned in the preceding paragraph. All these tribes were more or less related by trade, manners, customs, and dialect. Just prior to the advent of the whites upon the western coast of North America, as near as can be ascertained from the traditions of the Indians, the Chinooks were the dominant nation throughout all this section of the country. In 1850 they were on the decline, the smallpox having a few years before almost swept them away. Some of those then living were very old, and from them I obtained much of the history of the tribe and of the others that surrounded them. My knowledge of their language, which I could speak fluently, enabled me to learn during my sojourn among them many of their traditions, and much, not only of their own earlier life, but also of that of the other tribes composing the Chinook family.

An old woman, called by the whites "Aunt Sally," and who was the wife of the head chief of the Chinooks when Lewis and Clark made their first visit to that country in 1806, and is mentioned by them, well remembered their coming. I have spent many hours in conversation with her about the old times, listening with intense interest to her stories of "her people," as she always called the Chinook nation. She thought herself over a hundred years old, and perhaps she was right, but if so, she was a wonderful woman, for her mind was as clear and her memory as bright as those of two score less winters than those numbered by her. There were also old warriors in the other tribes, particularly among the Chehalis, Cowlitz, Klikatats, and Yakimas, who corroborated many of the stories and traditions told me by Aunt Sally.

The Chinook family consisted of many tribes, most of whom subsisted principally upon fish, the exceptions being those who occupied the mountainous country back from the Columbia River. The tribe living at the mouth of the river and along its banks to the distance of some fifty miles was known as the Chinooks, while the other tribes of the family had each a different name. The Cathlamets and Wahkiacums also lived in this section, but they were of the same general family.

Previous to the coming of the whites, the Chinooks were in the habit of going out to sea in their large canoes to capture whales, crossing the bar at the mouth of the river, a thing which in after years the best white navigators feared to do. After killing a whale with harpoons, they would tow it to Clatsop Beach, a long, wide, beautiful stretch of sand, just south of the river, taking advantage of the incoming tide to land it well up. Here they would make fast the harpoon lines to stakes driven in the sand, so that the ebbing tide might not carry their catch out to sea. As soon as the tide receded, all went to work at cutting up the prize, and when the water rose again there would be nothing left of the whale to be carried out. The process of fastening the whale on the beach was accompanied with no small amount of danger to life and limb. The coast proper was a ledge of perpendicular rocks, varying from twenty to forty feet in height, and if, while they were landing a whale, a tide came in somewhat higher than usual, it would sweep whale, Indians, and everything against these rocks, and as there were only a few crevices through which the Indians could climb to the top, it was a hazardous undertaking, especially if the wind blew fresh when the tide was running high.

Aunt Sally recounted to me that many Indians had lost their lives there ; and that at one particular time, many years ago, she went to the beach to see her people land a whale. There were evidences of a storm, and every available man and canoe had gone out to help draw the whale to the beach. The shore was crowded with women and children watching the operation. The hunters had towed the whale in so that it touched bottom, and were waiting as usual for the tide to rise sufficiently to enable them to pull it up and secure it where it would lie high and dry when the tide went out. Every time the whale floated they would tow it up a little farther, until they had it almost where they wanted to stake it ; when suddenly and without warning the wind changed to a terrific gale, and a tremendous wave swept in with such terrible force that it hurled the whale, the canoes, and the Indians helplessly against the ledge of rocks. The wave " poured over its own top," she said, capsizing and swamping the canoes, and dashing the occupants to their death against the jagged rocks. The water came over the top of the ledge in many places, and upwards of fifty of the men were drowned before the horrified eyes of their wives and children. She said nothing like it had ever been known before or since. When the tide went out the whale went with it ; but about a week afterwards they found it washed ashore some twenty miles down the coast.

The canoes of the Chinooks were of the same kind as those of the Haidahs, but after their numbers became so much reduced by disease the Chinooks ceased to make the larger sizes. They were made by burning and scraping, after the manner heretofore described. It took a man about three months to make a canoe that would carry three persons. Their weapons and fishing tackle were similar to those of the Haidahs. It was a very easy matter for them to live, as the Columbia River was filled with fish of all kinds, salmon and sturgeon being the largest varieties. With little labor they could catch enough salmon during their season to give them an ample supply through the longest winter.

It was their custom to catch and dry not only enough for their own use, but also a vast quantity for the purpose of trade with the inland and mountain tribes. Every fall they loaded their canoes with dried salmon and sturgeon, and quantities of hiaquas and went to the Cascades (the rapids of the Columbia River, about one hundred and fifty miles from its mouth), where they met the Indians from the mountains and plains and bartered their dried fish and hiaquas for slaves and for the skins and meat of the buffalo. They used the buffalo skins for making their summer wigwams, and their winter clothing and beds. The gray seal, beaver, and otter were abundant in and about the mouth of the Columbia and its tributaries ; and bear, panther, elk, and deer roamed the forests at will, but the Chinooks were fishermen, not hunters, and killed only enough of the land game to partially supply them with meat and skins.

The salmon is a fine fish, weighing all the way from ten to seventy pounds. The usual weight is from twenty to thirty pounds each. The Indians caught them with spear and net, as they cannot be taken with hook and line after reaching fresh water. Whenever we wanted to catch salmon with the hook, we were obliged to go outside the bar and a short distance into the ocean. There they would bite, and we rarely returned without a satisfactory catch.

In the olden times the Chinooks dealt very largely in slaves. Trading as they did with the inland Indians—who were much of the time at war with each other and, making slaves of their prisoners, desired a market that would take these slaves as far as possible from their native country,—the Chinooks had a fine opportunity to purchase and bring these slaves to the coast. There they sold them to the tribes both north and south, realizing a handsome profit, and becoming the wealthiest nation in all that part of the country.

Aunt Sally told me that when she was quite a little girl she accompanied her father, one of the chiefs of the nation, to the Cascades, on one of these trading expeditions. He purchased there a considerable number of slaves, among whom was a handsome woman about twenty years old. On the return trip this woman made two attempts to end her life by drowning; and after that the chief gave orders to have her bound every night to a tree, to prevent the accomplishment of her purpose. She was proud and high-spirited, and fully determined that she would not live to become a slave.

It had happened that two years earlier this chief had brought home a young man who spoke an entirely different language from that of the Chinooks and one that Aunt Sally as a child had never before heard. This young man was retained by the chief for his own use, and so it came about that the chief's bright little daughter saw much of the fine-looking young captive, and partially learned his, to her, peculiar language. When upon this first trading trip of Aunt Sally's she heard that one of the slave women had jumped into the river and been bound to a tree to prevent her doing it again, her girlish curiosity was aroused and she determined to go and see this strange woman. As she drew near she discovered that the captive was crying and talking to herself. Some of the words seemed familiar to the child, and to her great surprise she soon recognized them as words she had learned from the young slave of her father at home. As soon as she found that the young woman saw her, she began repeating some of the other words she had learned from the young man. The prisoner instantly stopped crying and gazed at her visitor in astonishment. She knew by the little girl's flat head that she was not of her tribe or any tribe she had ever been acquainted with. But the chief's daughter, by means of the words she had learned and by the use of the sign language which all understand, made known to the woman that there was a young man of her tribe at her father's home. The captive at once dried her tears, and afterwards made no further attempt at suicide, but sought by every means in her power to aid in accelerating the journey. On arriving home, Aunt Sally found the young man and brought him to see the new slaves. The young woman hesitated not a moment when she saw him, but with a little scream of joy bounded into his arms. It was her own husband, whom she had believed to have been killed in battle, two years before.

Sometimes slaves were permitted to buy their freedom; and through the persuasion of his little daughter, the old chief consented to give this young man the privilege of thus freeing himself and wife. Most gladly did he avail himself of this gracious offer, and with the love of his high-spirited wife to inspire him they were soon free. They were adopted into the Chinook tribe; for it was deemed by all an impossibility for them ever to reach their native country, on "the rising-sun side of the big mountains." The young man was the eldest son of the head chief of his tribe, and upon his father's death would have taken his place. Nevertheless he would always have remained a slave but for the kindness of that little girl who, when she told me the story, was a white-haired woman who numbered perhaps a hundred years.

Like all Indian nations who held slaves, the Chinooks treated them with harshness, even cruelty. Their services, their person, their lives even, were

9

the absolute property of their owners, and subject to their caprice. An owner might take the life of his slave without the slightest liability to punishment or question. Upon the death of one who owned slaves it was the usual custom to put at least one of them to death, to wait upon the master in the spirit land.

One day, while looking out upon the Columbia River, my attention was attracted by two Indian boys, who landed on the beach and drew their canoe up into the woods, whence they returned with boughs and tried to erase all their tracks in the sand. This proceeding excited my curiosity, and I determined to ascertain what it meant. I followed the boys into the woods, and after a long search found them hidden in the hollow of a tree. They were crouching down in a place scarcely large enough to hold one of them. Upon inducing them to talk, which I did with difficulty, I learned that they were slaves. Their master had recently died, and they were to be killed to serve him in the other world ; so, to save their lives, they had run away.

I took them to the house, put them up-stairs, and again seated myself at the window, to watch and await results. It was not long before I saw four Indians coming up the river in a canoe. They kept close to the shore, which they were apparently scrutinizing very carefully. When they reached the place where the boys had hauled up their canoe, the Indians landed, just as confidently as if they had seen the boys when they made their landing. What they saw to indicate the place I could not understand, as every vestige of the boys' visit had apparently been wiped out. They went immediately into the woods, and a short time afterwards I heard a rap at the door of the house. Opening it, I saw the four Indians, who told me of the escape of the slaves, and that they had traced them to my door. There was not the slightest use in denying this, for I well knew that Indians could track slaves like bloodhounds; so I said that the two boys had come to me, and that if they were slaves I wanted to buy them. They said they would not sell them; that they were the property of a chief who had died, and who was a brother of one of the four; that they wanted the boys, and would have them. After much discussion, and firm refusal of their demands upon my part, they became very angry, drew their knives, and threatened to kill me if I did not surrender the boys at once.

In the meantime I had stepped out of the house a short distance and planted my back against a tree, to prevent their getting behind me, and when they drew their knives I drew my revolver, telling them to put up their weapons or I would shoot. They knew what a revolver was, and quickly put their knives back into their belts. I then began bargaining for the boys, telling the Indians that under no circumstances would they be given up, but that I would pay them all they were worth in blankets; and finally offering ten blankets for each boy. I told them that was a high price for boys of that age, and that with such a number of blankets the dead chief could certainly buy two boys in the spirit land. My argument, backed as it was by a formidable-looking six-shooter, finally prevailed, and they accepted my terms. I gave them an order on a store not far away, where they went and obtained the blankets.

The chief was to be buried the next day ; and as it was only about thirty miles from where I lived, I went to see the burial. They cut five of the blankets into strips and wound them around the body of the dead chief, covering them by wrapping several mats over them. They then placed the body in a canoe the bottom of which was perforated with holes, and lashed another canoe, similarly perforated, over it. The whole was then conveyed to a platform which had been erected in the woods at some distance from the village, and which stood ten or twelve feet from the ground. After the body in its canoe-casket had been placed upon the platform, a fire was built near the place, and the remainder of the blankets together with many other things which had belonged to the chief were thrown, one by one, upon the fire, until all were consumed.

Their belief was that the smoke would waft all the burned things to the dead chief in the spirit land. The two boys were now safe, for they belonged to me, and no one had any right to touch them without my permission.

My brother was once travelling in the country of the Nootkas, and stopped overnight at a village where the people were mourning for the young son of the head chief who had died that day. He found

a slave boy about ten years old fastened to a stake
and awaiting the ceremonies which were to precede
his being put to death, to accompany his master's
little son to the spirit land. My brother succeeded
in purchasing this boy for five blankets and an ornament which he wore upon his watch chain. At the
burial they broke the ornament and placed the frag-
ments upon the breast of the little chief, and burned
the blankets. My brother brought the slave boy
home with him to the Columbia River.

It was the custom among all Indians to throw food
to their slaves, just as we do to dogs. If they failed
to eat all that was given the master would say : " If
you don't eat what I give you, it will be a long time
before you get any more." And so it would ; for
often he would not give them another mouthful for
two or three days. My brother arrived home with
his purchase, on the occasion mentioned above, just
before supper, and after the family had finished their
meal, the little fellow was seated at a table and
helped bountifully. My brother's wife, coming into
the room, saw that his plate was empty and had it
refilled. This occurred three or four times. The
last time, the boy said something to her which she
could not understand ; and calling to me she said :
" Do come here, and see what this boy wants ; I am
afraid he will kill himself eating." As soon as I
made my appearance he looked at me most beseech-
ingly. " Mammook nika muckamuck conaway
okook?" "Must I eat all this?" he asked in a
plaintive voice ; and when I told him he need not eat

any more than he wished now and should have all he wanted the next day, whether he ate this or not, he was greatly relieved and seemed very happy. This boy lived with my brother until he was eighteen years old when he died. He was a good and faithful boy; and he died a firm believer in the white man's God, and a true and devoted Christian.

The Chinooks believed in a good and an evil spirit of nearly equal power. These spirits had many contests as to which should control the destinies of the Indian, and therefore the Chinook was always striving to propitiate the one and appease the other. Hence, the attendance of good or bad fortune in his transactions determined in his mind which spirit was, for the time at least, most powerful.

Like many other tribes they believed that everything had its own spirit—the wind, the water, the thunder, the lightning, the trees,—all, according to their notion, had a spirit that governed them, as the spirit which occupies a man's body controls his actions. They could not understand how anything which has life or motion, as a tree that grows, water or wind that moves, or thunder that roars, can fail of having some inner life, or spirit, to cause the activities which they daily saw and heard. They also believed that great immovable objects, such as mountains, caves, etc., were possessed of a presiding genius.

As to the formation of mountains, rivers, etc., they believed that, in the long ago, the surface of the earth was quite smooth and level; that after dwelling long in harmony the different spirits quarrelled, and the water spirits were strong enough to sink portions of the surface for the rivers to run in, and larger portions for the lakes and seas to lie in ; that the spirits of the levels had power to hold their own in the contest; while the mountain spirits were vanquished and pushed up out of the way, and there obliged forever to remain.

In the early spring of 1854 I was spending some time in hunting in the Yakima country, and there became acquainted with an old Yakima from whom I learned many things regarding Indian life and beliefs in that section. He told me that when he was a child, his grandfather, then an old man, told him that he remembered perfectly well when the Columbia River at the Cascades ran under the land, and there were no rapids. In other words, there was a natural bridge across the river at that point.

Mount Hood, an extinct volcano, 11,226 feet high, lies to the southward of the Cascades, and but a few miles distant. Mount Saint Helen's is also a volcanic mountain, 9750 feet above the level of the sea, lying but a few miles northwesterly, and even yet occasionally emitting volumes of smoke. A legend told by the old Yakima was that the spirits of these two great mountains used to cross the river by this natural bridge to visit each other, until one day St. Helen's, in anger, shook it down.

The face of nature at and around the Cascades has not preserved any of the footprints of the spirits, but it has every other indication necessary to establish the truth of the story of the old Yakima. The banks on each side of the river at that point look as if they had been broken down, instead of being formed like the others along that portion of the stream. Just above the Cascades and for a distance of twenty or thirty miles may be seen acres of what was once bottom land covered with trees, now submerged to the depth of ten to twenty feet. The trees still stand there under the water just as they once stood in the primeval forest, except that their tops have been cut off to a level with the water by the ice.

This submerged land with its standing trees proves beyond question that, in the not distant past, the river was suddenly dammed at what is now the Cascades, and the water backed up over these lands. No one examining the place with care can arrive at any other conclusion than that at some time in the earth's history, and probably not much more than a century ago, there was a natural bridge there, and that it was probably thrown down by a volcanic eruption of one or both mountains, accompanied by an earthquake. The Indian's tradition, that Mount St. Helen's "got angry," indicates forcibly that the eruption took place in that mountain.

CHAPTER X.

IT has been charged that the Indians are a treacherous race. In the matter of warfare, or in transactions with one whom they believe would deceive or take unfair advantage of them, I think the charge can be sustained. They believe in the old adage that " All is fair in love and war." They have no scruples about making promises of good behavior for the purpose of drawing an enemy into an ambush or into some condition or situation where he would be at a disadvantage; but they will never betray a friend. I have known many instances where they have undergone hardships and defied danger to warn and protect their friends. One such instance related to myself.

And this brings me to the story of *Wah-kee-nah*— Wah-kee-nah the beautiful; Wah-kee-nah the fearless; Wah-kee-nah the true-hearted !

From 1850 to 1855 it was difficult in Oregon to get house servants, even at one hundred dollars a month, which was sometimes paid. During a trip into the Yakima country in 1850, my brother, of whom I have heretofore spoken, saw a bright, pretty Yakima girl—a daughter of one of the chiefs—of

some fifteen or sixteen years. She appeared so un-
usually intelligent and so perfectly neat withal, that
it occurred to him that his wife might teach her to
be very helpful about the house. So after getting
her consent to go and live with him at his home on
the Columbia River, sixty miles from her own
country, he gave her parents the same amount in
presents as if he was buying her for a wife, which
was much more than he would have had to pay
for a slave girl, and took her home with him. This
was Wah-kee-nah (signifying " most beautiful "), and
never was an Indian maiden more fitly named. In
face, form, and lissome grace she was peerless among
her race. We were all charmed with her. She was
apt in learning the duties of the household and of
great assistance to my brother's wife. I lived with
my brother at the time, and took great satisfaction
in teaching her English, while she was of valuable
assistance to me in learning her language. She lived
in the family for many years.

When Wah-kee-nah came to us she presented a
striking picture. She was dressed in the usual summer costume of the mountain Indian girl of that
section—a costume which disclosed rather than concealed her beautiful figure. About her waist was a
girdle some two and a half inches in width, and into
this were skilfully woven four rows of cords, made
from the fibre of bark and roots, which hung down
nearly to her knees and constituted her skirt. Her
only covering from the waist up was her very luxuriant black hair, which not only grew very thick, but

hung almost to her knees. If to the above be added the daintily embroidered moccasins which shod her feet, we have the entire costume—in which we first saw her. But she had that simple native modesty which saw no impropriety in such a dress. She had worn such a one as long as she could remember, and had never seen an Indian girl dressed in any other in the summer ; and it never had occurred to her unsophisticated mind that any girl could wear anything better or more becoming. My brother's wife immediately fixed up one of her own dresses for the young savage, and though she had considerable difficulty in persuading Wah-kee-nah to put on a " white woman's dress," she finally succeeded, and after that some new dresses were made for her, and Wah-kee-nah appeared no more about the house in the startling costume in which she came. When, however, she went to visit her own people she resumed her native costume, saying that all her friends would laugh at her if she wore the dress of the pale-face. Moreover, she continued to wear her own summer costume under her new style of dress for a long time and until she had learned to read and write. Then she began to take pride in being like white people, and adopted more fully the white girl's dress.

She looked very jaunty and handsome in her native winter costume. This consisted of a pair of leggins, made of buckskin, beautifully worked with beads and porcupine quills, and fastened around the waist. Over these she wore a skirt, also of buckskin and very elaborately embroidered, which reached a little below the knee and in shape was not unlike those worn by white girls. This skirt was also heavily fringed around the bottom. The costume was completed by a jacket, or waist, of embroidered buckskin, which in cut and shape was almost identical with the "surplice waist" of our own fashionable ladies in this present year of 1893. It was a very sensible and pretty costume.

Wah-kee-nah was a well-grown girl when she first came to us, but in her new life her tall, lithe figure rapidly rounded into superb womanhood. Her hands and feet were small and elegantly shaped, and her eyes, larger than is usual with her race, were very dark and lustrous. She was fleet-footed as a deer, and, while retaining all the quickness and alertness of the Indian, she soon added to these the grace of a queenly woman. She was an expert in the use of the bow and arrow when she came to us, but knew little of the use of fire-arms. In those early days in Oregon it was quite necessary that a woman, no less than a man, should know how to use the rifle and the revolver, and the ladies frequently joined in the sport of shooting at a mark with both these weapons. Wah-kee-nah often participated in the sport, and her keen eye and steady nerve soon made her an expert shot.

My brother's duties as Judge of the United States Court did not occupy the whole of his time, and he had taken up a claim of 640 acres on the north side of the Columbia River, and, after building his house upon it, had begun clearing up the land.

One day he accompanied the men who were cutting timber upon a distant part of the claim, telling his wife to send Wah-kee-nah with dinner for all hands about twelve o'clock. Wah-kee-nah was duly despatched upon this errand, but she soon returned to the house, saying that the Judge had told her to hurry right back and fetch him a rifle, as they had just seen a fine deer pass through the clearing. The girl was panting from rapid running and excitement, and all her Indian blood was alive at the prospect of the chase, while her eyes were fairly blazing with joyous expectancy. Her excitement was infectious. I caught it at once, and, giving Wah-kee-nah one of the rifles, I took another, and we started for the clearing. I was a pretty good walker in those days, but it gave me about all I wanted to do to keep up with this swift-footed and enthusiastic young huntress.

When we reached the clearing my brother told us that the deer had gone into the woods on the side towards the river, but he thought by careful pursuit he might yet get a shot at him. Wah-kee-nah begged my brother to let her go after the deer, as she had never yet had a shot at one. She was so anxious about it that I seconded her request, saying that if anybody could get him Wah-kee-nah was sure to do it. The Judge readily consented, and the girl started with a quick yet noiseless step into the woods. It was not very long before we heard the crack of her rifle. We started at once in the direction from which the report had come, but we could not find any traces of Wah-kee-nah. We called to her, but received no reply save the echo of her name. Concluding that if she had wounded the deer he would make for the river, we bent our steps in that direction, calling from time to time as we proceeded. After a time we heard her answering shout, and found her at the river's bank. She told us she had wounded the deer and had tracked him to that place, and that he must have swum over to the island. We could see for ourselves where he had gone into the water, for his tracks were plainly visible in the mud.

Wah-kee-nah was a splendid swimmer, and she at once proposed to swim over to the island after him. We tried to dissuade her from this idea, and induce her to wait until I could go to the house and get a boat; but she was so fearful that he would leave the island and swim to the mainland on the other side of the river; was so confident that she had wounded him; and pleaded so earnestly withal, that my brother finally consented to let her go. She did not waste any time. Divesting herself of her outer dress —thus leaving her attired in her Indian summer costume only—she tied her powder-horn upon the top of her head with the braids of her luxuriant hair. Then she put some bullets into her mouth, took the rifle in her left hand, and went quickly into the river. It was a stirring sight to see this fearless daughter of the forest buffeting with her superb dusky limbs the placid waters of the Columbia, while she held safely aloft her rifle with an arm that might well have served as a model for a sculptor. Not

Leander, eager to meet his beautiful Hero on the other side of the Hellespont, ever cleft the waters with stronger or more efficient strokes than did this Indian Diana swimming after her more humble prize. Steadily and quite rapidly she made her way to the island, and after walking a short distance along the bank she signalled to us that she had found the trail, and with her rifle ready for a shot began cautiously creeping into the underbrush, and soon disappeared from view. We waited quite a long time before we heard again the ring of her rifle, and then in a few minutes she appeared upon the bank with a glad shout and told us that she had killed the deer. I told her to wait there until I could get the boat and bring her home, and she seated herself contentedly on the bank to await my coming. It was a proud girl that met me and pulled the prow of my boat a little way up on the shore. Her eyes were fairly dancing with pleasure.

"What do you think of Wah-kee-nah now?" she said.

"Wah-kee-nah is a brave hunter," I said, approvingly; "but are you sure you have killed the deer?"

"Come and see for yourself," she answered with a laugh; and leading the way inland, rifle in hand (she had reloaded it immediately after shooting), she soon brought me to the place where lay her game. On the way she told me that her first shot had struck his shoulder and only lamed him; but the second shot had hit him in the head and finished

him at once. This proved to be the case. Her
second shot had entered just below and forward of
the left ear, and he could scarcely have made a move
afterwards. Together we dragged him to the boat,
and I brought Wah-kee-nah and her first deer in
triumph to the house. My brother's wife was warm
in her praises of the girl's prowess, and Wah-kee-nah
had a very happy afternoon.

But it was not very long after this episode that
my brother's wife had occasion to compliment Wah-
kee-nah again on her skill and daring; and this time
for an act that forever endeared the girl to the heart
of her mistress, and to all of us.

My brother's house was built upon a bluff, or
rocky cliff, on the bank of the river, some ten or
fifteen feet above the water at low tide. He had
built a picket fence around his yard and garden, to
secure the safety of the children. One day, however, his three-year-old boy found a loose picket in
the fence along the edge of the bluff, and crawling
through, tumbled over into the river. Fortunately
—or was it providentially?—Wah-kee-nah happened,
a moment afterwards, to come out of the house.
She did not see the little fellow fall over the bank,
but she did see the opening in the fence, and, being
no less prudent than she was brave, went at once to
fix it. As soon as she reached the fence she saw the
baby in the water. He was clinging spasmodically
to a piece of drift-wood, and being whirled round
and round in an eddy formed by some projecting
rocks. Wah-kee-nah grasped the situation instantly.

She did not faint with fear; she did not scream; she did not even run off for assistance. What she did was to tear off two more of the pickets with one sweep of her strong arms, and bound through the opening to the edge of the bank. Even as she reached it she saw the child lose his hold and sink beneath the whirling waters. But Wah-kee-nah never hesitated for a single instant. Marking with quick eye the spot where she wanted to strike the water, she made a " cut-water " of her two hands and plunged headlong into the river. The impetus of her falling weight carried her to the very bottom; but *she did not find the boy.* For one instant, her brave heart sank within her, as she thought that she had made a miscalculation. But it was only for an instant. The eddy had not permitted the boy to sink to the bottom, and as she looked up she saw him in the water almost directly above her head. Wah-kee-nah came to the surface with the child in her arms. He was partly strangled; but Wah-kee-nah, sustaining herself upon a projection of one of the rocks which was partly submerged, held him up in safety. The water came out of his mouth, the air revived him, and in a moment he was all right, and did not seem to be a bit frightened. Then she drew him around so that he rested on her back with his arms clinging tightly to her neck, and, swimming around the point of rocks to the little dock where the boats were kept, she brought the child all dripping to his mother, before she had even missed him.

The boy was not disturbed in the slightest degree by his perilous adventure. Wah-kee-nah had often given him his bath in the bathing-tub, where he would splash around in great glee. After his wet clothing had been removed and his mother had cried and laughed over him, and kissed and embraced him and Wah-kee-nah by turns, the little fellow started to run out-of-doors. When Wah-kee-nah intercepted him, he looked up at her, with his little, chubby face all aglow, and said : " Tub—Wah-tee, Kee-nah, tub—Wah-tee. Tome!" He wanted another bath in the great Columbia River, thinking it far more jolly than his tub.

This act of Wah-kee-nah's made a strong impression upon all of us. We fully realized that but for her bravery and alertness our little household would have been in mourning. Every one had been pleased with her before; but henceforth she was a member of the family.

Wah-kee-nah was always ready for any emergency, and her courage was unbounded ; indeed, it may be truthfully said of her that she was entirely without fear.

About the same time that my brother took up his claim, three or four other families also took up claims some three miles back from the Columbia River and in the valley of the *E-lo-ha-min*, a small river that emptied into the Columbia near my brother's house. They had cut a road following the bank of the river through the woods to their settlement ; but by going through the woods across the small spur of a mountain, a person could save about half a mile of the distance.

One of these farmers had an Indian girl to help his wife, and she and Wah-kee-nah frequently exchanged visits. On one occasion Wah-kee-nah went to spend the afternoon with her friend and failed to return at the usual time. We felt somewhat anxious about her as the time passed, but finally concluded that she must for some reason have decided to remain overnight, although she had never before done so without asking permission.

She came home quite early on the following morning, and we then learned the cause of her detention, and the story of her thrilling all-night experience. She had started early enough to reach home before dark, but stopped at the foot of the spur to pick berries. The time flew so fast that she did not realize how late it was, until suddenly she noticed that it was quite dark. Then she started in haste for home, but had gone only a little way when she heard the howling of wolves in the woods. As they seemed to be coming in her direction she hurriedly climbed a tree and seated herself upon a limb. It was but a little while before seven large mountain wolves made their appearance under the tree. None of us ever went into the woods in those days without a revolver, and Wah-kee-nah had not forgotten hers. She made prompt use of it, and shot the wolf that seemed to be the leader of the pack; but this did not frighten the others away. They were hungry and they kept prowling around the foot of the tree until it

became so dark that Wah-kee-nah did not dare to
come down and continue her journey. She had looked
in the chamber of her revolver after she shot the wolf
and found that there were but two shots left, and
she wisely concluded that she had better keep those
for use in case a panther or a bear should come upon
the scene and attempt to climb the tree. There was
nothing for her to do then but fix herself to spend
the night in the tree. So she climbed farther up
among the branches until she found a safe and comfortable seat, and there settled herself for the night,
with naught but the hungry wolves and the dismal
screech-owls to keep her company. She heard the
baffled wolves many times during the night, sometimes at a distance and sometimes under the tree,
scenting their dead leader. And thus this lion-
hearted girl of eighteen spent the summer
night. At daybreak, while stretching her tired limbs
into a more comfortable position, she caught sight
of another visitor creeping through the underbrush
towards her tree. The wolves had not been heard
for quite a long time, and it took but one quick
glance to assure the girl that it was a sleek and
sinuous panther that was approaching for this early
morning call. Wah-kee-nah glanced at her revolver
and saw that it was secure in her belt. Then she
prepared to give her unbidden guest a warm reception. With but two shots at her command she
could not afford to risk the chance of wasting even
one of them upon the panther while he was upon
the ground. There was no other tree near enough

for him to climb and thus spring upon her. He would have to climb her tree, and she must wait until he did it. But she had no notion of letting her unwelcome visitor select their place of meeting. She well knew that if he obtained a foothold upon a limb of the tree he could then spring upon her, whereas, while climbing the body of the tree he could make no spring. Lightly and very quickly she swung herself down to the lowest limb, and planting herself securely thereon with her head close to the body of the tree, pistol in hand, she waited his coming. She had not long to wait, for the panther wasted no time. As soon as he reached the tree, he, cat-like, began slowly and cautiously climbing it, while Wah-kee-nah's dark head hung over toward the side on which he came, as if to meet him half-way. Their eyes met—the panther's were eager, burning, fascinating,—but Wah-kee-nah's dark orbs were not disturbed. On came the panther, steadily, cautiously, but confidently. He had already covered half the distance between her and the ground, but Wah-kee-nah held her fire. As the brute came still closer and when she could almost have reached down and touched his paw, the girl glanced along her pistol-barrel. Her aim was at one of those burning eyes that had not left her own. A shot rang out on the still morning air, and an instant later the panther lay kicking feebly on the ground, while Wah-kee-nah still had one shot left !

But there was no need for a second shot. The aim had been true, and the panther soon ceased his struggles. Wah-kee-nah remained in the tree until after sunrise, to make sure that there were no more panthers or wolves about; then she came down, and soon reached home without further adventure. We had the animals skinned. Both were large and fine specimens of their species.

I come now to that story of Wah-kee-nah which is most intimately connected with my own life.

Just prior to the breaking out of the Yakima war, in 1856, I was hunting in the Yakima country, and knew nothing of the troubles that were bringing on a war. One night while lying wrapped in my blanket under a wide-spreading cedar and not yet asleep, I saw indistinctly some one approaching me. I felt rather nervous and apprehensive, for I had noticed for two or three days that the Indians had gathered in groups and engaged in earnest conversation, and that some of them seemed to look at me in an unusual—not to say uncomfortable—way. This had given me the impression that something was wrong, but I could not find out what it was. On asking them what made them talk so much and look so disturbed, they had told me that panthers were very numerous in the woods that year, and had killed a young chief of another village, and that they were worried on that account.

I had overheard something during the day that had caused me to discredit the panther story and to feel so disturbed that I could not sleep. So when I saw this nocturnal visitor approaching so noiselessly, I grasped and cocked my revolver. When the Indian had approached to within a few feet of me, I heard my name softly spoken in a voice that I recognized at once. My unexpected visitor was Wah-kee-nah.

I greeted her warmly and started to rise, but kneeling quickly beside me, and pushing me gently back, she put a hand softly over my mouth and told me to keep perfectly quiet. I obeyed her injunction, and she, remaining in such position as to have the appearance of a stump, to any one who might happen to be passing, told me in low tones of what had happened during my absence, and which she said had determined her people to take the war-path. The outbreak she said was very near at hand; in fact the Yakimas were only awaiting the return of the head war-chief, who had gone on a mission to some of the neighboring tribes to get them to join in the war, and that they would begin killing the whites as soon as he came back; and that if I remained there I would probably be the first victim. I felt that Wah-kee-nah was right. I knew that the sagacious girl was reliable in her information—indeed it was fully corroborated by my own observations. I was a good deal excited, and saying I would go at once with her, started to rise. But once more she placed her hand firmly upon my shoulder and said " No." She explained that it would not do at all for us to go away together; and that we would be almost certain to be discovered, in which case the lives of both would be forfeited. Even should we be able to travel unseen for the remainder of the night, my absence, she said, was sure to be noticed early in the morning, and pursuit and death would certainly follow. "We could kill some," she said; "but there would be too many for us; and besides," she added, "I don't like to shoot my own people."

I saw the full force of what she said, and could not doubt that her views were correct. "But what is to be done?" I asked. Then this simple child of the mountain forest unfolded to me a plan so simple and yet so feasible for my getting away, that when I heard it I wondered why I had not thought of it at once. She said I must be sick in the morning, not so sick that I could not ride, but sick enough to demand the care of my white doctor, and must tell the Indians that I would have to go to him at once, but would return in a few days and finish the hunt. I must not, she said, on any account remain in the village another day. Even while Wah-kee-nah was telling me this, I had outlined in my own mind just how I could carry out her plan, and I felt no little exultation in the thought that my safety was assured, unless the war-chief should return before I got away, which was not probable, as Wah-kee-nah said they did not expect him under two days. Then it occurred to me that Wah-kee-nah herself was in great danger; for should her tribe learn what she had done they would surely kill her. I told her this, and that I could not let her go alone. But she promptly reminded me that these were her own people, whom she was in the habit of visiting quite frequently, and added quite naïvely that her only danger was in being seen with me.

" That is true," I said ; " I will do what you say ; and now you must go quickly."

" Yes," she replied ; " I shall see you at home day after to-morrow." Then with a noiseless tread she stealthily vanished from my sight in the thick wood.

I watched her lithe, retreating figure as with swift, noiseless footsteps she disappeared in the thick darkness of the wood. Then, for the first time, I fully realized what she had done,—how much she had risked for me,—and my heart was very full. It is nearly forty years since that February night when I lay looking up at the stars whose coy glances twinkled through the cedar branches, and the blood does not course as swiftly through my veins as in those earlier years. But I have not forgotten that on that night I wiped away a silent tear as in my inmost soul I breathed a fervent prayer that the good God who created all races of men would watch over and protect the savage maid whose form had just mingled with the shadows.

The hours seemed long before morning came, for I was ill at ease, and sleep but dallied with my eyelids. I think I never felt better physically, however, in my life, but I soon grew desperately sick. And in order that I might look it as well as act it, I took the precaution to swallow some tobacco ; and any of my masculine readers who remember their experience in learning to " chew," will realize that I not only looked sick, but felt so. The Indians seeing how very pale I looked, began asking me what was the matter. I told them I had been taken very ill in the night and must go to a doctor. They at once offered to summon their medicine man, but I said I knew what was the matter, as I had been troubled with such attacks before, and the white doctor always brought me out all right. So, I said, I would go to him, and his medicine would fix me all right in two or three days, when I would return and finish the hunt. I saw them holding a long council, lasting until into the afternoon before any one went to bring me a horse ; but finally they brought one, and it is needless to say that I made good use of him until I reached the river. There I took a canoe and arrived home in safety on the following morning, where I was welcomed with great rejoicing. It is perhaps unnecessary to add that I did *not* return to finish the hunt in the Yakima country.

It was only after my return that I learned the details of Wah-kee-nah's coming to me in the woods. She undertook to rescue me from my imminent though unconscious danger entirely upon her own motion ; and when she had made her plans she confided her intention to my brother and his wife, and received from both their hearty approval. This noble girl paddled a canoe up the river thirty miles, and then travelled about twenty-five miles through the dense forest, on foot and alone, to save my life.

This incident, though it is more than usually striking by reason of its principal actor being a girl, is but a typical illustration of the depth and sincerity of Indian friendship, of which, as I have said before, I have known numerous instances. It is upon such acts that I found my belief that there does not exist upon the face of the earth a race that is less treacherous or more true to a friend than the Indian.

My readers will naturally want to know what became of the beautiful Indian girl of whose life I have sketched some of the leading incidents, as I knew them.

A little while before the breaking out of the Yakima war,—from being possibly the first victim of which Wah-kee-nah so heroically rescued me,— the eldest son of the head chief of the Yakimas, a fine-looking young Indian, named Le-lim, came several times to see Wah-kee-nah. He courted her assiduously, but she always refused his offer of marriage. I asked her one day why she did this. Her dusky cheek flushed a little richer red as she replied : "I do not want to leave my pleasant home. I am happy here. I like the whites better than the Indians, and if I ever marry I want to marry a white man."

When the war broke out all friendly communication between the Yakimas and the whites was naturally broken off, and I saw no more of the handsome young chief. I left Oregon immediately after the war ; but I learned that Le-lim soon after renewed his visits to Wah-kee-nah. He was a persistent lover, and evidently one who believed that " Faint heart never won fair lady "—or Indian maid. His unremitting and earnest wooing finally brought its great reward. He won for his bride the peerless beauty of his tribe, and Wah-kee-nah returned to her own people the wife of the chieftain's son.

I know not whether now she be living or dead; but I do know that never a whiter soul, never a braver heart, were incarnated than the heart and soul which dwelt in the beautiful body of Wah-kee-nah. When this little volume leaves the press I shall try to have it find her if she be living, or find her descendants if she shall have gone to the spirit land; for I would like to have her know, and have them know, that years have not dimmed the memory or blunted the gratitude of the friend for whom she risked her life; and that he pays her this sincere and loving tribute.

CHAPTER XI.

WITHIN a day or two after my return from the Yakima country, as narrated in the foregoing chapter, the Indians began murdering the white settlers, thus inaugurating the Indian war which took place in Oregon and Washington territories in 1856, and was known as the Yakima war. It was brought on by causes similar to those which have occasioned every other war between the Indians and whites that I have ever known or heard of. But it has been said that the Indians themselves began this war—that they struck the first blow, and were therefore clearly the aggressors. Yes, without doubt—the *immediate* aggressors; but only after they had submitted to outrages and villainies on the part of the whites, until patience ceased to be a virtue and further endurance was impossible.

Major-General John E. Wool, who commanded the forces of the United States in this war, says in his official report to the War Department :

"If one half the money appropriated for the Indians in California had been properly and judiciously expended, it appears to me we would have had no trouble with them."

Speaking of the hanging of an Indian by a party of whites, he uses this strong language : " The sub-Indian agent ought to have been arrested and confined for permitting or sanctioning so great an outrage."

Referring to a certain settlement of white men, he remarks : " The Indians living near there are continually exposed to the brutal assaults of drunken and lawless white men ; their women are assaulted ; and if the assault is resented, the Indians are beaten and often shot. So great is their dread that, upon the approach of the whites, the women run to the mountains and hide until the whites have left. A great many cases of ill-treatment might be mentioned and they are so common here as scarcely to excite comment. If there had been the same desire to do justice to the Indians and to maintain peace, that there was to make war and plunder the Indians of their lands, horses, and cattle, we should have been relieved of all trouble, and the United States of a very large expenditure of money."

In regard to a case in which the Indians had killed a white man, he says : " I will simply remark that the death of Sub-Agent Wright was caused by an old grudge against him for attempting, before he was appointed Agent, to poison a whole band of Indians."

Noticing further the causes which had led the Indians to take up arms, he says :

" Another source is the outrages which are committed on the persons of friendly Indians, from revenge or mere wantonness. A few days since, an old Indian was most wantonly shot in the town of Steilacoom. . . . Not long since, two Indians who had been arrested and were in chains, were shot down in Olympia. These several murders have caused great excitement among the Indians. . . . Three friendly Sno-qual-a-mie Indians were atrociously murdered near Seattle, and one at Mound Prairie."

The extracts quoted are all from the General's report to the Secretary of War. I personally know of some most inhuman and outrageous murders. In one case, a father and mother were shot down while defending their daughter from the assaults of two white men.

These disgraceful and inhuman atrocities make a bad showing for the settlers of those territories. There were as good people residing there, however, as ever inhabited any part of the globe ; but it must be remembered that the gold excitement of 1849–50 had drawn to the Pacific Coast a vast number of adventurous and lawless men,—a horde which the better element was totally unable to control during the first few years; and when these outrages were committed, the law-abiding citizens were absolutely powerless to arrest and punish the perpetrators. These lawless men had no settled home, and when they committed a crime, if they saw the smallest probability of punishment they would mount their ponies and go to some mining camp or other place where they could not be found.

By the Indians the whites are all regarded as brothers. We are all as one great tribe to them. Hence if a white man killed an Indian, the Indians considered it perfectly proper and just to retaliate by killing any white man who fell into their power, without regard to his having had any direct connection with the crime against them. This of course could not be tolerated by the white settlers. They could not be disinterested spectators to the murder of some innocent citizen in retaliation for the act of a lawless, wanton scoundrel. Had the Indians confined themselves to seeking out and killing the miserable villains who had injured them, there would have been no war. But looking at the matter from the Indians' point of view, can we fail to see that, according to their lights, they were fully justified in making war? The whites suffered heavily in this war; but it resulted, as all Indian wars have resulted, in greater disaster to the Indians themselves. First and last, they have always been the greatest sufferers.

Indian wars have always been fraught with terrible calamity to the white settlers in their vicinity; for, when on the war-path, Indians are cruel and without mercy, and death is much to be preferred to falling alive into their hands.

Many heroic deeds and hair-breadth escapes occurred among the settlers during the Yakima war. One which I will relate illustrates the fortitude and courage of woman in the face of deadly peril.

A man who was living on a ranch some six miles

distant from the nearest village, in order to secure
the safety of his wife and daughter, started to go to
the village to make arrangements for moving them
there before the war should reach his section. He
had been gone from the ranch but a short time,
when his wife saw ten Indians all in war paint (which
was a *sure* indication of their purpose) approaching
the house. This woman and her sixteen-year-old
daughter were accustomed, like most women in that
country, to handling the rifle, and they each seized
one and fired upon the approaching warriors. The
weapons had been well aimed, and two of the
Indians bit the dust. The others fled precipitately
to a piece of woods back of the house and about
three hundred feet distant, and began firing their
arrows into the windows. The women kept good
watch, and whenever an Indian showed himself they
fired on him. In this way they succeeded in killing
two more of their foes during the afternoon. The
Indians tried to set fire to the house with fire-
arrows, and just at nightfall succeeded in doing so.
But the brave mistress of the beleaguered house was
equal to the emergency. She promptly gained the
roof and extinguished the fire, her courageous
daughter bringing the water to her. During this
time the mother received an arrow in her side, but,
regardless of the pain, remained on the roof till the
fire was out ; she would undoubtedly have been
killed but for the partial darkness.

Coming down from the roof, the women fired
several shots into the woods to let their besiegers

know they were still in fighting trim. Then under cover of the darkness they, each with her trusty rifle, crept stealthily out of the house by the front door, keeping the house between them and the Indians until they reached the woods. They groped their way through the thick darkness of the woods, until they reached a little stream which they knew ran through the village, and following this, reached the village about daylight the next morning.

A party immediately started to learn the fate of the husband, and found that this band of Indians had met him shortly after he left the ranch, and had killed him. His body was found on the road about two miles from his home, pierced with arrows. There was every indication that when he became aware of the presence of the Indians he had turned his horse and attempted to get back to his family. The prints of the horse's feet were plainly visible in the road, first going toward the village at an easy gait, then back for about half a mile, on a run. How he became apprised of the presence of the Indians and how they could kill him, he being mounted and they on foot, can only be conjectured ; but the probability is that he was ambushed.

The mother's wound was not very serious, and she soon recovered. After they had left the house the Indians burned it—probably setting it on fire again with fire-arrows, and consoling themselves with the thought that they were avenging the death of their four brother-warriors, by the roasting of the two plucky women whose prowess had sent them to the spirit-land. I looked at this little mother with perfect astonishment while she was telling me her story, and marvelled greatly that so much courage and " clear grit " could exist in so frail a body.

The sufferings of the whites during Indian wars are well known ; but there is no record of those of the Indians. They have no hospitals to care for their wounded, no anæsthetics to relieve pain. If their sufferings during the war, and those caused by the whites in times of peace could all be told, they would show an aggregate of misery that could not fail to wring pity from a heart of flint.

A Chehalis Indian (who had not joined in the war, but had with others moved close to a white settlement in order to be known and recognized as friendly Indians) told me that one day his wife with her three children, the eldest a boy of ten, went into the woods to pick berries. While there two white men came along and assaulted her. While she was struggling with them her boy struck one of the men with a stick no thicker than a man's thumb, whereupon the wretch drew his revolver and shot the little fellow, the ball entering his shoulder and passing down into his body. The poor boy lived eleven days, suffering the most intense agony. While the stricken father was telling me this story, the tears coursed down his cheeks and his body trembled from head to foot. " My poor little boy, how he suffered !" he said ; " Oh ! my poor little boy !" and his voice was stifled in sobs. My own eyes were wet as I listened, and thought of the sufferings endured by that poor little child during those eleven long days before death mercifully came to release him. The brave little fellow's only crime was that he had sought to defend as best he could the mother he loved from the brutality of a " civilized " white man.

One more story from the many tales of wrong and suffering that came to my knowledge must suffice.

I was riding one afternoon with three friends, and when about six miles from the village we saw an old broken-down horse feeding by the side of the trail. His back was very sore, and one of our party made the remark that any one who would use a horse until he was in such a condition ought to be punished. While talking, we heard a groan, and, moving on a little farther, came upon an Indian lying on the ground, and apparently in great agony. I asked him what had happened, and he told me that he had that morning met here a white man riding the old horse we had just seen. The white man told him he wanted to trade horses with him, but as the Indian had a good horse and the horse the man was riding was good for nothing, he said he would not trade, and rode on toward the village. But he had gone only a few paces when the white man shot him in the back. He fell from his horse, which the white man then mounted and rode away. I examined the wound and found that a large pistol bullet had entered his back just under the shoulder-blade, and passed entirely through his body. I ascertained that his home was about seven miles distant, and when I told him that I would go and inform his people, he seemed greatly pleased. So we made a bed of grass and laid him carefully upon it, and while my friends remained to watch over him, I rode off to his wigwam. When I arrived there I inquired for his brother, and as soon as he came, related what had happened.

His expression I shall never forget. Intense grief and anger were so mingled in that dusky face that it photographed itself indelibly upon my mind. He called to one of the women not far away, and a few brief words apprised her of what had occurred to her husband. She cried aloud in her great grief, and her two children joined in the crying.

Then four Indians mounted their ponies and, leaving the weeping mother and children, followed me at a rapid pace back to the place where I had left my friends and their charge. But the wounded man was beyond human aid. He had died only a few minutes before we reached the place. They wrapped the body in a blanket, and putting it upon one of the ponies, bore it back to the widowed mother and her children. I draw a veil over the scene at that wigwam; and it is needless to attempt to put in words the feelings toward white men which such cowardly butchery would naturally inspire in the hearts of the family and tribe of the victim.

We tried to ascertain who it was that had committed this most cowardly murder. It was believed to have been a Mexican, who had been for a day or two in the village, and who was travelling from one mining camp to another. A party started out upon his trail the next morning, but after following it for two days, came back unsuccessful.

Volumes have been written regarding " Indian atrocities," and the "red devils" who perpetrated them have been painted as without mercy and without feeling; as fiends incarnate ; but the whole damning story of *white atrocities* against the Indians must forever remain unwritten. The Indians wrote no history, had no literature ; but they were not devoid of human feeling and a sense of justice. They knew and remembered the bitter wrongs of their race, and, so far as they could, avenged them.

CHAPTER XII.

THE marriage ceremony differed considerably among the various tribes composing the Chinook family. In one which I witnessed near the Columbia River, the groom had made his proposal to the maid of his choice, aged about seventeen; the usual presents had been proffered and accepted; and all was in readiness for the wedding when I arrived in the village. The groom opened the ceremony. He was dressed in gala costume, and carried a blanket. This he threw on the grass at a short distance from the wigwam of the bride and seated himself upon it with an expression upon his face as melancholy as if he was there to be shot. He was soon surrounded by his friends; but this living circle was left open on the side nearest the wigwam of the bride. She soon appeared in front of the wigwam, looking very pretty in a costume which comprised all the finery she possessed. Standing there a few minutes until all her family and friends had joined her, she started at a slow pace toward the groom, who now looked, if possible, more dejected than before. Her friends followed her closely in procession, all chanting monotonously, while the bride walked in silence.

When about twenty feet from the groom the little procession came to a halt, the bride keeping her eyes steadily fixed upon the ground. Then the groom's party began chanting, and one of their number stepped forward and presented a blanket to the chief master of ceremonies, the father of the bride. Following this presentation the bride's party joined in the singing, all chanting in chorus, while the bride tripped briskly forward to the groom and seated herself beside him at his left hand. Then the father of the bride, advancing with stately tread, threw the blanket that had been given him over the heads of the couple, covering them completely. Up to this time the groom had not raised his eyes from the ground; but whether he continued to remain so demure while under the blanket I will not presume to say.

As soon as the bride's father resumed his place among his own party, the chanting of both parties became louder, and all began dancing around the couple in the most fantastic style. After about ten minutes the chanting and dancing came to an end, and both parties formed a line, the groom's friends upon the right and the bride's upon the left. The father of the groom, who was master of ceremonies for his side, then advanced and removed the blanket that had covered the "happy pair," and while they were still sitting made a speech of some length in which he recited the principal duties of a wife to her husband, and those of a husband to his wife. Both listened with downcast eyes, but it was noted that

the groom had lost his melancholy expression under
the blanket, and I thought I caught a little twinkle
in the bride's shy eyes. When the speaker had
finished he uttered a loud guttural sound—a sort of
Indian " Amen."

Thereupon the husband and wife (as they now
were) arose. The groom's father placed the blanket
which had covered them upon the shoulders of the
bride and the other blanket upon the shoulders of
the groom. Then, stepping out in front, he gave
the signal and all started for the groom's wigwam,
the newly married pair marching between the two
lines. On arriving at the future residence of the
couple they halted, and the groom's father raised the
door of the wigwam. Quickly turning, the bride
sprang lithely upon the back of the groom, and, amid
the most vociferous chanting of all present, was
carried by him into his wigwam. As soon as they
had crossed the threshold the father dropped the
curtain, and all dispersed, to gather later in the
afternoon and participate in a feast at the home of
the newly married. In the early evening I paid my
respects, and had quite a chat with them. They
seemed very happy. This was a " marriage in high
life," and I was informed that it was purely a love-
match.

The ceremony I have just described was a very
pretty one ; but of a far more exciting nature was
an engagement and marriage I once witnessed among
the mountain Indians. The tribes living near the
Columbia River did their travelling in canoes, and had

but few horses; but the mountain Indians had many
horses and were expert riders.

It sometimes happened that a very pretty girl,
especially if she were a chief's daughter, would have
many suitors vying with each other for the possession of her heart and hand.   Occasionally duels grew
out of such rivalry, but this was not of frequent occurrence, as the older people usually managed to avert
so serious a termination of affairs, by proposing some
game of chance or deed of daring, in which he who
won should also be the winner of the maiden.   In
other words she became the high stake for which they
contended.

In the case I now speak of, the maiden was a
chief's daughter and a beauty. She had four suitors.
They had each been sending presents, and these were
all accepted by the parents, which signified that so
far as they were concerned there was no preference.
It was the custom, however, to return all gifts except
those from the suitor who should win the girl.   A
chase on horseback was proposed as the method by
which the contest should be decided—the maiden to
marry the lucky man who should catch her in the
race.

This most exciting love-chase took place on a
bright June afternoon. The Indian village where
the chief lived was located at the base of the mountains, in a beautiful grove skirting the large prairie
where the ponies fed.   The girl was allowed to make
her choice of horses, and she selected one that she
thought the fleetest—a fine black; and as I carefully

looked at the animal it seemed to me that she had chosen wisely. The young men had their own horses. It was agreed that the maiden should be given several minutes, before the young men should be allowed to start.

I made inquiry as to which one of these young men was supposed to be favored by the chief's daughter, and was informed that it was he with the bay horse. He was a handsome young warrior and the most intelligent-looking of the four, though they were all fine specimens of athletic youth. The girl looked very handsome mounted upon her spirited black. She was attired in the usual summer costume of the mountain Indian girl which showed to advantage her large and well developed figure, but she had put on also a closely fitting and beautifully embroidered buckskin jacket, and her heavy black hair was braided up and confined closely to her head. As she rode at an easy pace out over the prairie, she looked an object well worthy of pursuit; but there was a determined look in her snapping black eyes as she rode away which indicated that this was to be a very real race.

When the time came for the pursuers to mount and start, I gave special attention to the bay horse, and was annoyed not a little to see the rascal commence bucking the moment his rider was on his back. By the time he started the others were far in advance. But the girl was evidently looking over her shoulder to see how matters were going, and when she saw the bay so far behind she began adroitly to guide her horse in a circle which would naturally give the bay a chance to "cut across" and get even with his competitors; but they were all too far ahead to have this ingenious little scheme succeed to any extent. The others quickly changed their course, and the girl was about being intercepted, when she turned and ran her horse at the top of his speed towards the upper end of the woods.

Her horse was much the best runner, and she was able to keep them all at a distance, unless the black should tire under her—it being an undoubted fact that a woman can never get as much work out of a horse as a man is able to obtain. I was on horseback, as were many of the Indians, and we hurried to the upper end of the wood when we saw her evidently making for that point.

But when she reached the wood she seemed to find the trees so thick as to impede her progress, and her pace slackened to a slow trot.

On came her pursuers, two of them far in advance and nearly abreast of each other. It is a critical moment. They are gaining upon the girl at every step, and now but the distance of a few rods separates her from the triumphant grasp of a man for whom she has no love. Alas, unhappy maid! and alas, thrice unhappy rider of the treacherous bay; your happiness is lost! You must helplessly see another win the prize your prowess should have gained! It is now only a question of which of the two leaders shall secure a beautiful though unwilling bride. My heart stands still in pity. The black horse and his rider seem to make no progress in the thicker wood, while their pursuers are rapidly lessening the intervening space.

Forward they dash, neck and neck, each horse and rider straining every nerve to be first at the side of the steaming black and his beautiful rider, now but a few yards ahead. At this juncture the sorely pressed maiden casts one swift glance over her shoulder. Never shall I forget the expression of that face. Her dusky cheeks are tinged a deeper red, her teeth are tight set, while her full red lips are drawn over them in a straight hard line; and her eyes! surely it is no look of *despair* that blazes out from those dark magnificent eyes! What can it mean? In an instant she had reined her horse a little to the left, and passed between two great trees into what was nearly an open space beyond. A moment later, and the full import of her look became clear to me.

Upon either side of the narrow opening through which she had so deftly passed, the low-growing branches of the great trees and the thick underbrush formed for some distance an impenetrable barrier. *The opening between the trees was not wide enough for two horses to pass abreast!* The two eager suitors evidently realized the situation, but the prize for which they struggled was the flower of Indian beauty; their blood was up, and neither would give way. They urged their horses to their utmost speed, and both rode straight at the opening. In the par-

tial turn that had to be made, the rider on the left
gained a slight advantage, and it seemed for one
brief moment, as his panting horse put his nose between the trees, that he would slip through ahead.
But what he had gained in distance the rider on the
outer curve had gained in momentum. With a terrific yell he drove his horse right into the narrow
opening! There was a crash, mingled with yells of
rage and pain, and men and horses went down together in a helpless struggling heap. Two of the
lovers of this plucky girl were effectually disposed
of. Woman's strategy had scored its first great
triumph in this remarkable race.

According to the Indian idea, it would be a re-
proach and a disgrace should she allow herself to be
caught without, apparently at least, making every
possible effort to avoid it ; so she must now seem to
elude the one to whom she would willingly surrender, no less than those by whom she would not
be caught. The bay and the gray on which the
two remaining pursuers rode were very evenly
matched, and at this moment emerged from the
woods and came riding down upon her, nearly neck
and neck, and not an eighth of a mile away. But
she was ready for the race, and not only kept good,
but widened, the intervening distance. She had a
clear head and a quick eye, and if her horse held
out, was evidently mistress of the situation. With
two of her lovers disabled in the woods, she seemed
easily able to elude the other two.

At times she would run in a circle, and if one of

her pursuers started to cut it she would whirl and
go the other way, very much to his discomfiture
and the advantage of him who had held to a straight
course; so they both became very chary about
cutting corners. This part of the race was all upon
the level open prairie, and this beautiful young
savage won warm admiration by her equestrian dash
and daring. It seemed that her pursuers could not
outrun her, and they certainly could not out-
manœuvre her. There was an understood rule
applying to such races, that after the lapse of a certain time—about an hour—the girl might, if she
chose, return to the village, and if she arrived there
without being captured by any of her pursuers, she
was safe, and the lovers were laughed at unmercifully. Whether because she noticed that her horse
was tiring or because she had had enough of it for
herself, the heroine of the present contest concluded
to end it by taking advantage of this rule. So,
watching a favorable opportunity, she started straight
for the village. Both lovers divined her intention
and both urged their steeds to the utmost. The
girl glanced backward and saw that the gray horse
was a little in advance of the bay, and then she plied
her whip fast and furiously. But the black *was*
getting tired, and now showed it very plainly. Again
I became anxious and excited. It looked as if, after
all the strategy and daring displayed by this spirited
girl to enable the man she loved to win her, he was
now going to fail at the last moment; and, what was
worse still, it seemed more than probable that she

would fall into the hands of the unloved suitor. Both were gaining upon her, but the gray horse was now at least ten feet ahead of the bay. Just as I had given up all as lost, I saw the gray stumble and fall. He had stepped in a hole, and being on so keen a run and nearly exhausted, had been unable to regain his balance and fell, throwing his rider flat upon the prairie. A quick glance over the shoulder revealed the situation to the flying girl. She was still more than a quarter of a mile outside the safety line, and she did not cease to ply her whip; but I thought that I could see that the blows had grown lighter, far lighter than they were when both men were in pursuit; and while apparently urging her steed to the utmost, she was overtaken by the bay a few rods outside of the safety line.

As he came up beside her he put his strong right arm around her waist, and gently, but very quickly, bore her from her horse and seated her in front of him upon his own; and the black horse came in without a rider, while the bay bore a double load.

Had this race taken place among white people, the excitement would have been wild, and the enthusiasm unbounded. The grove and the village would have rung with shouts and cheers. And it would have been the same with the Indians but for my presence. There was evident pleasure shown by the friends of the man who won his bride, but there was no shouting or cheering. This illustrates a striking phase of the Indian's character: they repress all signs of emotion when in presence of the whites.

The wedding took place on the following afternoon, and the ceremony was quite similar to that among the river Indians, described earlier in this chapter. The following are the points of difference. In this case instead of all the friends forming a ring and dancing around the couple while under the blanket, they formed a double line and marched slowly seven times around the couple, devoting each round to a particular spirit, and chanting an invocation to him.

The first round was to propitiate the Great Spirit, and in the chant they implored him to be always with the bride and groom and to do them good.

The second round was to appease the Evil Spirit, the chant beseeching him to do them no harm.

The third round was to the Spirit of the Woods, that he would furnish them with game in abundance.

The fourth round was to the Spirit of the Water, that he would guide the fish into their nets.

The fifth round was to the Spirit of the Air, that he would give them wild fowl in plenty.

The sixth round was to the groom, that he would be good to his wife.

The seventh round was to the bride, that she would be good to her husband.

Should anything unpropitious happen during the marching of the procession, it was supposed to augur that the spirit in whose round it occurred would not be friendly to the young couple. Should the unpropitious omen occur during the round for the groom the procession at once halted and the master of ceremonies in behalf of the bride advanced to the couple and, raising the blanket, told the groom what had happened, and then put the direct question to him: "Will you be good to her?" and if he answered affirmatively the evil omen was thus counteracted, and the march and chant were continued. Should the omen occur during the round to the bride, the groom's master of ceremonies proceeded in the same way, asking her if she would be good to her husband, and her affirmative reply had the desired effect.

The chanting during the bride's round was done entirely by her friends, who extolled her virtues and goodness in the highest degree. In the round to the groom, his friends did the chanting in his praise. When the march and chant were finished, the ceremony proceeded to the end as with the river Chinooks.

My readers will see that this was an exceedingly elaborate as well as a very beautiful ceremony, taking place as it did in the open air, and on the soft green turf under the light of the glad sunshine, the fantastic and brilliant costumes of the participants made it most picturesque, while the solemnity and decorum with which it was conducted made it very impressive.

This, however, was the ceremony for people in high life. The more humble were married by mere agreement or by purchase, in which case, when the price had been paid, and when the so-called gifts were satisfactory, the man took the girl to his home and she was thenceforth his wife. No further ceremony was required.

The presents were sometimes given in instalments, the young man not being able to furnish all at once; and in such cases he could not have his bride until the last article had been delivered—there being no credit extended in matters connubial.

Owing to their mode of life and their training from childhood, all Indians possessed wonderful sagacity and acuteness in many things.

It was exceedingly difficult to follow them through the woods when they did not wish to be followed. They usually, in such cases, sought a stream and walked in its waters in the course they wished to pursue, until some rocks were found upon which they could step and walk for quite a distance. The sun and wind would soon dry the rocks, leaving no trace to indicate where they left the water. If, on the contrary, they desired to be followed by friends, they would leave many signs. They sometimes stripped the outer bark from a tree near which they had camped, and with hieroglyphics informed the following party of all that had occurred, and also the course they intended to pursue. The most common mode of giving the information, however, was by driving a stick with two splits in its top into the ground at every place where they camped, and placing two pointed sticks in it. The upper stick pointed to where the sun was when they left; if before daylight, it pointed down to where they supposed the sun to be at the time; if in the day, it pointed directly toward the sun, so the following party would know just how long they had been gone, if it was the same day. If longer than that, they judged by the appearance of the ashes and footprints, and generally correctly. The lower stick pointed in the direction they had gone. Then, as they passed along, they would break a twig or branch here and there, making it point in the direction they were going. If they changed their course, they would break two branches near together, one pointing like the others, the other in the direction to which they had turned.

The knowledge of this last sign was of good service to me at one time. A friend and myself were once in the forest far from civilization, hunting elk, with Indian guides. One day, when quite tired, we told the guides to go on and we would follow when we were rested. They told us to come to a grassy knoll, some three miles beyond, and there wait, as we would camp there. After resting, we went to the knoll. Here we saw many fresh signs of elk, and in a conspicuous place found a split stick driven into the ground, the upper pointer showing that our guides had left there about an hour before, the lower one giving us the direction. I had lived with the Indians long enough to understand that they wanted us to follow them, instead of remaining there, and we did so, shouting occasionally at the top of our voices. We found little branches broken here and there, and had no difficulty in following. In about an hour and a half we received a reply to our shout, and soon found our guides skinning a fine elk. They said they wounded him while he was feeding at the grassy knoll, and had tracked him all that distance before getting a final shot. Feeling confident that they would get him, after his being so badly wounded, and knowing we should want to camp wherever he fell, they left the directions for us to follow.

Gambling, as I have said before, was the great vice of the Indians. It prevailed among the Chinooks, as well as with the other tribes inhabiting this section of country.

I was once travelling in my canoe, and seeing a good camping-place, had my Indians paddle to it for the purpose of camping for the night. On reaching it, I found some eight or ten Klickatat Indians there. After supper I went over to their camp. Several of the men were gambling with a set of beaver's teeth. They at once commenced bantering me to join them, which I declined to do. After a while, one of them brought his wife, a very pretty young woman, and challenged me to have a game with him, he to put up his wife as a wager, against my canoe. This generous offer I also respectfully declined. He had a fine set of beaver's teeth, all smoked, marked, and properly dedicated to the deity of good luck. I tried to buy them of him, but he did not wish to sell. He offered to play a game with me for them, I to put up the value of four beavers' skins (four dollars). I hesitated, for I feared losing my four dollars. The Indians began bragging about their skill, and jocosely taunted me as to the white man's lack of it, until finally I felt called upon to defend the honor of my race, and at it we went. For-

tune favored me, and I won the beaver's teeth.   I
gave him the four dollars, however, (which was all
the teeth were worth, except in his imagination, as
he believed them to be an especially lucky set) and
we parted good friends.

This universal passion for gambling which exists
among all Indians, arises I think, chiefly from two
causes: first, the prevailing belief in fate, luck,
chance, or whatever it may be termed—that unknown *something* which each believes will come to
him in whatever he undertakes and bring him success; and second, the abundant leisure which the
Indian's indolent life leaves on his hands.   Naturally
he seeks some diversion for his idle hours, and his
mind turns easily to games of chance.   Games requiring skill and bodily exertion do not interest him
so much.

I have witnessed a great deal of gambling among
the Indians, yet I never saw a quarrel over any
game, nor have I ever seen one Indian attempt to
cheat another.   In their play Chance is the divinity
they worship, and they submit loyally to his edicts.
The loser will accept his fate with true Indian stoicism, even if he lose his all—an example which the
gambling fraternity of the white races might do well
to follow.

CHAPTER XIII.

O F the four grand geographical divisions into which for convenience I divided the Indians of North America, two have been considered; and we will now return to the Atlantic coast for the purpose of taking up the consideration of the third division, which embraces all those south of the thirty-third parallel of north latitude and east of the Rocky Mountains.

It seems quite certain that Columbus was not the first European who discovered the great Western continent, as the Norsemen undoubtedly preceded him by some four hundred years. But without any unnecessary discussion on that point, it suffices to say that it was the discovery of Columbus that gave an impetus to settlement, and therefore, whether first in point of time or not, his was the first discovery that was followed by any practical results.

In 1508, Ponce de Leon, a Spanish discoverer, visited the island of Porto Rico, and after procuring considerable gold from the natives, sailed for home. But not being satisfied with what he had procured by barter, he returned the next year with an armed force, and reduced the defenceless Indians to vassalage, ruling with great severity, and robbing the natives of everything of value which they possessed.

In 1512 he left Porto Rico, and landed upon the continent of North America. He arrived upon the coast on the twenty-seventh day of March, of that year, but did not land until April 2d; and because he found the country so fair and beautiful, it being in its finest verdure, and arriving there on Palm Sunday, the Spanish name for which is "Pascua Florida," he called the country "Florida," which name it has ever retained. Some authorities hold that he was the first discoverer of that country, discrediting all others laying claim to that distinction.

He was received with great kindness by the Indians, and spent several months cruising around the coast, in search of the "Fountain of Youth," which he believed existed somewhere in the New World, and in whose wonderful waters he hoped to bathe and become young forever. In return for their kindness he, on sailing for home, forcibly captured and carried away several native men and women.

The next year he returned at the head of an expedition for the purpose of reducing the Indians of Florida to the status of vassals, as he had those of Porto Rico. In this, however, he was unsuccessful, and not until 1521 did he again make his appearance, and this time he brought a much larger force. But he was met with determined hostility, the Indians gathering their forces and fighting with such tact and bravery that he could not even land. In one of the attempts to do so, he received a wound, which resulted in his death a few days afterwards, and thus his scheme to subjugate the Indians of Florida came to an inglorious end.

In 1520, one Lucas Vasques de Ayllon, a Spanish officer of some distinction, landed on the Florida coast, and was received with great kindness by the Indians. He made feasts, gave the Indians gifts, and made every profession of friendship. By these means he enticed one hundred and thirty of the natives on board his vessel, locked them under hatches, and sailed for Spain, intending to reap a large profit by selling them as slaves. But his inhuman project ended in disaster. Two of the vessels floundered at sea and went down with all on board. The other arrived in Spain, but he received no profit from the sale of the Indians, because they nearly all died of grief. Exasperated at his lack of success he determined to try again. It was not until 1524, however, that he succeeded in procuring three vessels. These he loaded with soldiers, intending this time to do away with all artifice and carry out his project by force of arms. Arriving on the coast, he landed, and was again received with great kindness and hospitality by the Indians. The Indians affected great cordiality and pleasure at his return. They had taken from him a lesson in " civilized " diplomacy, and they had learned it well. They were so friendly as to completely disarm De Ayllon of suspicion, and he congratulated himself upon the ease with which he was going to accomplish his purpose. While enjoying this feeling of security, and laying his plans for future action, he sent a party of two hundred soldiers some distance back into the country for the purpose of spying out the land. The Indians entertained and feasted them there for four days, and then suddenly and unexpectedly attacked and put them to death, not leaving even one to tell the tale. They then made a vigorous assault upon the Spaniards at the coast, killing the greater part of them. The few who were able to reach the ships quickly made sail and left the coast. De Ayllon was numbered among the slain.

The Indians had well learned the lesson of duplicity and treachery he had taught them. They had visited upon him terrible retribution, and glutted their vengeance for the loss of the one hundred and thirty of their nation, who had been stolen by him upon his first voyage, and whose death he had ruthlessly caused.

It seems, as near as can be ascertained from the traditions of the Indians, that during the century just preceding the coming of the whites, there were many powerful tribes inhabiting the territory which I have called the third grand division. I shall only mention such, however, as possessed some peculiarity, or among whom has occurred some incident worthy of special notice. The Iroquois had overrun some of the territory lying between the Atlantic Ocean and the Mississippi River, below the thirty-third parallel, and held some of the tribes living there under tribute; but, in the main, the tribes inhabiting this vast region were independent and strong. They were not so

warlike or brave as their northern neighbors. Climate
had much to do with this. The bravest and most
warlike tribes were located where the weather was
neither very hot nor very cold—either extremes
seemed to enervate and weaken the race. Had
the Indians inhabiting this section of the country
been like the Iroquois, the Shawnees, the Sioux, or
other tribes in their division, the Spaniard Narvaez
could not have marched through their country as he
did in 1528, with only three hundred men and eighty
horses. At first he was kindly received, but his conduct and that of his men so enraged the Indians
that they soon became his enemies. They did not
annihilate his force, however, (as the northern Indians
would certainly have done) although they had from
the fourteenth of April, to the twenty-second of
September in which to accomplish it. The Spaniards
finally became discouraged and left the country in
some boats of their own construction, and all perished
except five—Cabeca de Vaca and four others—Narvaez being among those who succumbed to the
vicissitudes of the voyage.

It was during this expedition of Narvaez that
there occurred another instance of a woman's successful plea for mercy somewhat similar to that of Pocahontas. The Indians captured Juan Ortiz, a young
man only eighteen years old. The chief ordered him
to be killed, as he was terribly enraged against the
white men for the injuries his mother had received
at their hands. While the preparations were in
progress for putting Ortiz to death, the daughter of

this chief, who was about the same age as the prisoner, threw herself at her father's feet and pleaded so earnestly for the captive's life that the old chief reluctantly consented to spare it. Some months after this it happened that his life was again in jeopardy, and his girl deliverer again interposed, warned him of his peril, and advised him to flee to Mucoso, a neighboring chief of the same tribe, and in the darkness of the night took him some distance on his way, placed him in the right path, and, giving him a true woman's blessing, with kind wishes for his welfare, bade him waste no time. He reached Mucoso in safety, and was protected by him. The maiden was affianced to this Chief Mucoso, which accounts for the white prisoner's being so well received.

The next white man to come into this territory was De Soto, who landed upon the western coast of Florida on the twenty-fifth day of May, 1539, with about one thousand men and three hundred horses. From some captured women De Soto learned that a white man was a prisoner not far away, and, guided by them, a party of horse started in search of him. They met him making his way to their camp. We can only imagine his feelings upon thus meeting a party of his own countrymen, after having been a prisoner among the Indians for twelve years, with scarcely a ray of hope of ever again reaching his native land.

De Soto remained in the country for three years, going up and down through it in search of gold, which he and his followers believed to exist somewhere in that section in great quantity, and as they

could not get the Indians to tell them where it was,
(except a little in the mountains of what is now the
State of Georgia) they sought for it unremittingly
until, exhausted with the fruitless effort, they were
forced to abandon the search. `

During these three years De Soto treated the Indians with the utmost brutality, supporting his thousand men and three hundred horses by robbing the
corn and vegetable fields during the summer and fall,
and in the winter he would make raids and seize all
the grain and vegetables that the Indians had laid
up for their own use. Many Indians starved to death,
because every particle of food they had secured for
winter use was taken by De Soto's soldiers and carried away to their camp, not leaving even a vestige
for the Indians, whom they knew could not exist
without it. De Soto also captured a large number
of Indians and compelled them to carry all the baggage of his army. If any one of them refused to
carry his load, a chain was put around his neck and
he was dragged, either by four or five men or by a
horse, until he was dead, or would consent to get up
and have the load lashed upon his back.

De Bry, who wrote an account of De Soto's jour-
neyings, says that at one time they took many women,
and that the captain selected two or three of the
handsomest for the commander, and apportioned
the others to himself and the rest that went with
him. He also relates that on another occasion the
Spaniards found two Indian men and one Indian
woman gathering beans, and that although both the

men might have escaped, one of them, the husband of the woman, would not leave her, but fought most bravely and to the death to protect her.

In the course of his wanderings, De Soto came to the country of a woman chief, who is described as young, beautiful, and amiable. Upon De Soto's approach, he was met by an ambassadress, a sister of her majesty, who delivered a speech of welcome. In a little while the queen came out, borne upon a chair carried by her courtiers, who brought her to a river, upon the opposite bank of which De Soto was encamped. Here she entered a large canoe, and, accompanied by numerous other canoes containing her principal men, was taken to De Soto's camp. On arriving, she landed and presented De Soto with rich presents of skins, and also a beautiful string of pearls which she took from her own neck; after which she cordially invited him to enjoy the hospitality of her country. He accepted the invitation, and was handsomely entertained for some time. On his departure, he repaid her kindness by robbing the graves of the dead of all the pearls that had been buried with them, and making the queen herself a prisoner and holding her as a hostage for the good behavior of all the Indians. After remaining in captivity for several days, and being taken a long distance from her own country, she one day out-witted her guards and escaped. It is said that one of the Spaniards assisted her in this, and went with her to her own country.

After a battle, in which the Indians had shown much courage and which had cost the lives of some

of his men, De Soto took all the chiefs he had captured, and with an axe severed both hands from their
arms at the wrists. The surgeons tied up the arteries,
so as not to let the poor sufferers have the relief of
bleeding to death, and then allowed them to return
to their families handless and helpless. At another
time he had one hundred prisoners tied to trees and
shot. At still another time he captured three Indians, and, because they did not tell him where he
could find gold in the fabulous quantities he expected, he caused one to be tied to a stake, and, in
in the presence of all, slowly burned to a crisp, in the
hope of thus extorting the desired information from
him or from the others.

And who was it that committed all these atrocities
upon a simple people whom they found originally
not only inoffensive but hospitable and kind? It
was men who called themselves Christians—men
who, as their first act upon landing on these shores,
raised and planted the holy cross, a symbol of the
blessed religion of Jesus Christ, a religion of love,
mercy, and justice. Men who had with them twelve
priests,who, every morning and every evening, erected
an altar around which De Soto and all his followers
bent the knee to Him who taught, " Do ye unto others
as ye would they should do unto you "!

When we see men like these, professing to be
civilized and even Christianized, committing such
cruel atrocities, how can we blame the poor unedu-
cated Indian for the cruelties practised by him, when
he had never had the advantages of civilization or

even heard of the sweet, justice-loving religion of our Saviour?

De Soto did not live to return to his native land. He was taken sick with a fever on the banks of the great Mississippi River, and died on the twenty-first day of May, 1542, at the early age of forty-two years. Had he lived until the twenty-fifth day of the month, he would have been in this country just three years His followers, fearing the Indians would desecrate his body in retaliation for the many wrongs he had done them, should they bury him on land, wrapped him in his mantle, and, by the dim light of the stars, conveyed him to the middle of the river, and secretly buried him beneath its waters.

After the death of their leader, the only desire of the followers of De Soto was to return to their native country. At first they tried to reach Mexico by following the course taken by Cabeca de Vaca, but becoming discouraged, they returned to the Mississippi, and built seven large boats, forging the iron bolts, nails, etc., which were required in building them, from " the chains they had for leading the Indians." They then floated down the Mississippi River to the Gulf of Mexico, and coasting along to the westward, finally reached a Spanish settlement called Panuco. There were only three hundred and eleven survivors of the thousand men who three years before had landed upon that coast. All their horses that had not died from exhaustion had been killed for food, and the expedition left the country without having found the gold they sought, broken and dispirited, but leaving behind them a track of bloodshed, heartless cruelty, misery, and death. Had the Indians an historian to record the sufferings inflicted upon them by these civilized savages, the record would indeed be a most dreadful one.

The Spaniards made some further attempts to explore Florida, notable among which was that of De Luna, in 1559. His force was composed of fifteen hundred soldiers, and a large number of friars and preachers ; but his expedition, like all the others of his countrymen, ended in failure.

In 1562, when Charles IX. was King of France, Admiral de Chastellon was the head of the Protestant party, and conceived the idea of founding an empire in the new world, which might afford a refuge for the Huguenots should it ever become expedient for them to leave France. He fitted out an expedition consisting of two vessels, and placed it under the command of Captain Jean Ribaut, an officer of much experience. Ribaut landed upon the coast of Florida, near what is now the village of St. Augustine, but almost immediately sailed to the northward, and entered the River St. John, which he named the "River May," that being the month in which he discovered it. Here he erected a monument, upon which he engraved the arms of France. He then continued to sail northward until he arrived at the harbor which is now called Port Royal. Here he erected a fort, in which he placed twenty-five men under the command of Captain Albert, and supplying him with an abundance of ammunition and provisions, returned to France.

The French in their dealings with the Indians adopted a policy which differed very widely from that of the Spaniards. They were cordially received, and returned the Indians' hospitality with kindness. Fairbanks says : " The French seem to have a peculiar faculty of ingratiating themselves, and had most remarkable success in conciliating and securing the friendship of the Indians. The secret consists most probably in the peculiarly adaptable and versatile talent of the French, enabling them to accommodate themselves with ease to any customs or usages, and putting them at once at home wherever they may happen to be placed. Another reason is, that they are skilled in the art of pantomime, the only language at all available upon first meeting with a tribe whose language is unknown. The Frenchman, with his varying gestures, his expressive shrug, his flexible features, his animated manner of expressing himself, would soon be on a good footing, and smoking a pipe with the chief, where the stately Spaniard would be expressing his pleasure in pure Castilian, and making gestures at the end of his lance ; or the Englishman, with his phlegmatic temperament, would be attempting a direct negotiation."

Whether this explanation be correct or not, it is a fact that the French had far less trouble than other nationalities with the Indians. But the French attempts to settle in Florida met with dire disaster. The inhumanly brutal Spanish leader, Mendez, after inducing the French to surrender under promise of protection, tied their hands behind them, and cruelly butchered them all.

CHAPTER XIV.

THE Indians of Florida suffered many vicissitudes, as that country became a battle-ground between the French and Spaniards in the earlier years, and afterwards between the Spaniards, British, and Americans, until finally it fell permanently into the hands of the Americans. The Miccosukies were the most powerful tribe of Florida Indians in the earlier days, and the Seminoles, an offspring of the Miccosukies, in the later time.

William Bartram, a celebrated botanist who spent a long time in their country, thus writes of the Seminoles in 1773:

"They possess all of East Florida, and a large part of West Florida, countries which, divided as they are by nature into innumerable islands, hills, and marshes, marked by many rivers, lakes, streams, and vast prairies, offer a great number of desirable localities convenient for settlement. This country, so irregular in its form, and so well watered, furnishes, besides, so great a quantity of the means of subsistence for wild animals, that I do not hesitate to say that no part of the world contains so much game and so many animals suitable for the support of man.

Surrounded with this great abundance, the Seminoles are contented and happy, and are as free from
care as the birds. They present a picture of perfect
happiness. The only disquietudes they entertain,
are caused by the continued progress of the white
settlements."

Although this was written in 1773, it would probably have been a good description of the nation in
1508, when Ponce de Leon first arrived among them ;
but as no one had then penetrated their country, to
tell us how they lived, we shall never know ; yet I
think we have a right to conclude that they *must*
have been as contented and happy a race then, as
they were found to be nearly three centuries later.
How different was their condition after the war
which lasted from 1832 to 1840.

Oseola was the leading chief of the Seminoles
during this war with the United States. The white
settlers were clamoring for their lands, and the
United States proposed that the Seminoles leave
Florida and go to lands west of the Mississippi
River.

Oseola, who was then thirty-one years of age, opposed the measure most bitterly. At a conference
held with the Indians by General Thompson of the
United States army, for the purpose of negotiating
a treaty by the terms of which they were to abandon
their lands in Florida and accept lands in the West
in return, Oseola became angry, and in the greatest
excitement drew his scalping-knife and driving it with
great force into the table upon which the treaty lay,

said : " The only treaty I will ever sign, obliging us
to leave our lands, is with this."

He proved a most powerful enemy, but was captured toward the close of the war by the bad faith of
General Jesup, who violated the usages of civilization by seizing him when he came in under a flag of
truce to negotiate a settlement of the difficulties.
General Jesup excused himself by claiming that
Oseola was an escaped prisoner, he once before having been in the hands of the whites and having made
his escape. He was confined in Fort Moultrie at
Charlestown, South Carolina, where he soon became
dejected and low spirited, and gradually pined away,
even unto death.

Much has been written of this renowned chief of
the Seminoles. He was possessed of noble traits of
character. His manner was dignified and courteous,
and upon the field he proved himself a brave and
gallant leader. He always instructed his warriors to
spare women and children. He said, " It is not upon
women and children that we make war and draw the
scalping-knife, it is upon men, and let us act like
men." Unfortunately for the whites his instructions
were not always obeyed by his followers.

He died while yet a prisoner at Fort Moultrie, and
we are told by eye-witnesses that a short time before
the end came he seemed to realize that he was
dying, and although unable to speak, he made known
by signs that he wished his wife (who had been permitted to remain with him) to dress him in the
clothes he always wore at war councils, to gird on

his war-belt and lay his bullet-pouch, powder-horn,
and scalping-knife beside him. He also asked for
his red paint and looking-glass, which she held before
him while he deliberately painted one . half of his
face, neck, throat, wrists, backs of his hands, and the
handle of his knife, a custom practised by his tribe
when the irrevocable oath of war and destruction is
taken. He then placed his knife in its sheath under
his war-belt, and carefully arranged his turban upon
his head, with the three feathers he was in the habit
of wearing in it. Being thus prepared, he rested
for a few moments to recover strength, and then indicated by signs that he wished to see the other
chiefs who were prisoners with him, and also the
officers of the fort and his two little children. Just
before they arrived, he had his wife bolster him up
in a sitting posture, and when they came in, he, with
a pleasant smile, extended his hand to each of the
officers and chiefs, and shook hands with all in silence.
Then turning to his wife and little children he bade
them a most affectionate farewell ; after which he
signalled to be laid down upon his bed, which was
done. He then slowly drew his scalping-knife from
his war-belt, and holding it firmly in his right hand,
quietly folded his hands upon his breast, and, without a struggle or a groan, died with a smile upon his
face.

It will be remembered that the war originated in
the attempt of the whites to compel the Seminoles
to vacate their country and migrate to lands west of
the Mississippi River ; and the policy of the United

States all through this long war was to send all the prisoners to those lands. In this way the number of the Indians was reduced to the merest remnant. These hid in the swamps, and from their hiding-places would sally forth occasionally and do much damage.

Many murders and not a few hair-breadth escapes grew out of these raids of the Indians. One most exciting adventure happened to the family of Dr. Henry Perrine, a celebrated botanist in the employ of the United States government, who was living on an island called Indian Keys, lying near the coast of Florida. He was under the impression that the Indians would not disturb the people on that island, and therefore made no preparations for leaving. I have the narrative from the Doctor's son, Mr. Henry E. Perrine (Mrs. Grover Cleveland's step-father), who is now living in the city of Buffalo, New York. His father's family had lived upon the island but two years, and at the time of the attack consisted of his father and mother, two sisters and himself. He was thirteen years old, and vividly remembers everything that occurred.

About two o'clock on the morning of August seventh, 1840, the family were awakened by the sound of muskets, and the yells of Indians. Dr. Perrine's house stood upon the beach, and what was usually the cellar in other houses, was an excavation into which the sea water could flow through an opening in the wall leading directly under the wharf. This wharf was covered with planks, but the sides were

walled with stone for some distance from the house,
and the part leading out into the deep water, had
sticks driven around the sides and end. The sticks
were also placed across under the wharf in front of
the walled portion, thus separating the space under
the wharf into two parts. The front part was used
as a turtle corral.

When the yells of the Indians became louder, and
it was evident that they were approaching the house,
Dr. Perrine hurried his family down through a trap-
door into the water, saying, " I will go back and see
what I can do," probably intending to get his Colt's
rifle, which was good for sixteen shots. His son
then remembered that on his last hunt he had used
every one of the cartridges, and called to his father,
telling him so ; but he answered, " I know it, but I
will see what I can do." His father then put the
trap-door over the family and drew a large chest
over it. The family waded through the water to the
hole in the wall leading under the wharf. It was
high tide, and there was only a foot of space between
the surface of the water and the planks above their
heads, the water being about four and a half feet
deep. It was not long before they heard the Indians leaping upon the wharf directly over their heads,
and they held their breath for fear of discovery. He
heard his father talking to them, after which, hearing
nothing more for awhile, he supposed the Indians
had gone away. Soon, however, the loud yelling
commenced again, and they heard the Indians bat-
tering in the doors and windows. Then they heard

a voice say in English, " They are all hid, but the old man is up-stairs." This proved that there was a renegade white man with them, and such were known always to be much more savage and brutal than the Indians. They soon heard a terrific pounding on the door leading to the cupola, and after a fearful crash came most vociferous yells and shouts, which proclaimed to their listening and affrighted ears, the death of the husband and father.

For a long time after this they could hear the Indians dragging things out of the house upon the wharf, and loading them into canoes. At one time, one of the Indians raised the trap-door of the turtle corral and looked in, but the partition of sticks prevented his seeing the frightened and trembling refugees, who were in the other part. They were in breathless suspense while he was looking, fearing their white night-clothes would reveal their position. Some hours after daylight, the smoke came rolling in under the wharf where they were, and they began to hear the crackling sound of flames, which indicated that the house was on fire. The tide was then so low that there was only a few inches of water under their end of the wharf, and the smoke became so dense that they were almost suffocated. They held their mouths near the surface of the water, and drew their breath through their wet clothing. The wharf also caught fire, and they could see the little tongues of flame eating through between the planks over their heads. Seeing that they must be burned if they remained there, young Henry made a desperate at-

tempt to break the partition, and finally succeeded
in getting through into the turtle corral. Looking
through the crevices between the piles and seeing
that all was quiet, he quickly raised the trap-door,
got upon the wharf, and dropped into the water. It
was now low tide, and he waded around the point
and over to the other wharf, not far away, looking for
a boat which he knew was kept there. He found it
already half filled with plunder by the Indians, who,
he afterwards learned, were at that very time in a
store not two hundred feet away, occupied in gathering goods to put into this very boat. On looking
up, he was delighted to see that his mother and sisters had also forced their way through the partition,
and scrambled out of the trap-door. It was now a
little past noon, but they could not possibly remain
under the wharf any longer, as the live coals were
beginning to fall on them from the burning planks.
They had plastered marl over their hair and shoulders, as best they could, to keep from being burned ;
but one of the sisters will bear upon her shoulders to
her dying day the scars made by the burning coals.
Henry told them of the boat, and guided them
around the point, wading in the water all the way,
as that was the quickest way of reaching it. His
sister Sarah, who had been so ill that she had not
left her bed for two weeks, now became exhausted
and said she could go no farther, and begged them
to leave her and save themselves. But that, of course,
they would not think of doing, so they supported
her until they reached the boat ; then gently laying

her down in it, his mother, his other sister, and himself pulled the boat off the shore. In it they found one oar, one paddle, and two poles, and with these they pushed, pulled, and paddled for dear life, toward a schooner out in the bay. The Indians soon discovered them, gave chase, and came near overtaking them before the people on the schooner saw them. As soon as they were seen from the schooner, a boat was lowered, and the men pulled toward them with powerful strokes, knowing the lives of the refugees depended upon their reaching them before the Indians. As the pursuers were on the point of overtaking them, the men in the boat opened fire upon the Indians, which caused them to turn and flee ; and that brave little thirteen-year-old boy placed his mother and sisters safely on the vessel's deck.

This is one of the incidents that show how *young* our Republic is, for that heroic boy now walks the streets of the city of Buffalo every day, hale and hearty, and is far from being an old man. Mr. Perrine says that when he thinks of it, the whole scene comes before him as vividly as if it had taken place but yesterday.

This attack was made, as before stated, in 1840, after the Indians had been pursued by the army for eight years and had become desperate and in great need of almost everything, and, as there was a fine store on this island, they probably made the attack more for plunder than for murder. The house, shop, and negro quarters of a Mr. Howe were not burned, and Mr. Perrine says the reason for that was uncertain, but it was thought to be because before the war, when the Indians were in the habit of coming to the island to trade, Mr. Howe lived there and had treated them kindly and thus won their friendship.

Had every one pursued such a course with the Indians, how different would have been the history of the settlement of this country!

These Indians had not come to the island during the war, and therefore Dr. Perrine was unknown to them.

The United States government, in 1841, finally compromised with the few Seminoles still remaining in Florida, and agreed that they should remain there upon a small reservation, but that none of those who had been transported west of the Mississippi River should be allowed to return, so that only a few hundred now occupy the reservation. Yet they are so proud that they despise the whites, and will have nothing to do with them except in the way of necessary barter and trade; they will not allow a white person to live on their reservation, and are so tenacious of their blood that, should one of their nation intermarry with one of the detested white race, they would kill upon sight the unworthy Seminole who had thus brought disgrace upon them all, and their laws would sanction the murder.

Between the Mississippi River and the Rocky or Sierra Nevada Mountains lived many tribes. Some of them, as the Konzas, the Pawnees, and some others, had the singular custom of cutting all the hair from the heads of the men, with the exception of the scalp-lock. In the early days, before the introduction of knives, they burned off the hair with hot stones, always leaving a patch at the top of the head some three inches wide and four inches long. The hair upon this spot they would tend with great care, making it grow to the greatest possible length. They usually wore it braided, hanging down the back, and ornamented with paint and feathers. It was a disgrace to have this hair cut short, for it indicated, in their estimation, a lack of courage not to have a good long scalp-lock for an enemy to bear off as a trophy. With some of the tribes this custom was universal, in others it was only occasional, while in others still it did not exist at all.

This section of country was most beautiful, being divided into prairies and timber land in convenient proportion; and in 1832, when Mr. Catlin passed through it, it seemed to be alive with buffaloes and wild horses, bands of both being visible every day. There is no animal on the prairie so wild and sagacious as the horse, and none more difficult to capture. His eye is so keen that he can see an enemy at a great distance, and when once started he does not stop for several miles. Mr. Catlin made many attempts to paint pictures of these horses while they were grazing or playing. He never succeeded except in a single instance, and that was when he crept through a ravine for two miles, with the wind blowing from the horses toward him; and then, from the shelter afforded by a little hedge of bushes, which effectually screened him, he was able to make a fine sketch. He says: " They were of all colors, some white as milk, some jet black, others sorrel, and bay, and cream-color, while some were pied, having a variety of colors on the same horse. Their manes were very profuse, and hanging in the wildest confusion over their necks and faces, while their long tails swept the ground. I do not know of a prettier sight than a band of wild horses at play. I have watched them through a glass, which gave me a fine view, and sometimes joined the Indians in the chase, and attempted to lasso them, but generally with very poor success personally, but the chase was exciting, and seeing the Indians catch and tame them, interesting."

I have had some of the same experience, with about the same personal success, but as Mr. Catlin says, riding with the Indians while chasing and catching them is exceedingly exciting.

The Pawnees were a large tribe who, since the advent of the whites, have devoted themselves more to agriculture than any other tribe in this section. As early as 1828, they had large fields of corn, pumpkins, squashes, and beans, and with a great abundance of buffalo-meat easily obtainable were amply supplied with food.

The Kioways, another tribe inhabiting this section, were distinguished from the others, as they were a much finer-looking race of men and women. They were tall and erect, with a great abundance of hair, so long in many cases as to nearly reach the ground.

It is a curious fact that the flattening of the head, as practised by the Chinooks heretofore described, prevailed in this section among the Choctaws and Chickasaws, and not among the adjoining tribes. Here, some two or three thousand miles from the Chinooks, with not a tribe between them practising the singular custom, we find it prevailing in two large tribes and accomplished in the same way and for the same purpose ; and another fact that should be mentioned is, that there is not the slightest similarity in the language of the Choctaws or Chicasaws to that of the Chinooks, whence the theory, that the one may have been an offshoot of the other, is out of the question.

The Comanches, a large and powerful tribe, also inhabited this section of country. They lived in large villages containing as many as six or eight hundred lodges, or wigwams, covering from three to four thousand persons. They built them almost entirely of skins drawn over poles in the way I have described in connection with the Sioux. They were very much like the Sioux, and were adepts in tanning skins and making them soft. They were also expert horsemen. They did most of their fighting on horseback, throwing themselves upon the opposite side of the horse while at full run, and thus protecting themselves from the enemy's arrows.

They were offshoots of the Shoshonees, of whom I have spoken as inhabiting the country farther to the northward. All travellers who visited them in their primitive state give them a good character. Among such I would cite Rev. Mr. Parker, Lewis and Clark, Captain Bonneville, and Mr. Catlin. The latter says: " I allege it to be a truth, that the reason we find them as they are usually described, a kind and inoffensive people, is that they have not as yet been abused—that they are in their primitive state, as the Great Spirit made and endowed them, with good hearts, and kind feelings, unalloyed and untainted by the vices of the money-making world."

This was in 1832, and without doubt he spoke truly in relation to their character; and yet, from reading the reports of the wars that have taken place between them and the whites since the white man began to crave and settle upon their lands, driving the Indians from them, we might suppose the Comanches were Devils incarnate; for they have fought like heroes for the protection of their homes and firesides.

Alas for them, civilization has planted her iron heel upon them, crushed them into submission to its dictates, and crowded them into the narrow limits of a few reservations, upon which to eke out a miserable existence, dependent upon the honesty (?) of Contractors and Indian Agents.

CHAPTER XV.

A T a time preceding most of the events herein narrated that transpired upon the Atlantic coast in that part of the country now known as the United States of America, the Spaniards were engaged in making voyages of discovery, and some expeditions had landed on the coast of the southern portion of North America, in a country called by some of the natives Anahuac, and by others, Maheco, which latter name was changed into Mexico, the name which it still bears.

In 1519, when Hernando Cortes first visited this country, it was inhabited by various tribes of Indians, all classed, however, as Aztecs, who were more advanced in civilization than any other Indians upon the continent of North America. All but one or two of these tribes were subjects of the powerful monarch, Montezuma.

Cortes, on his way to Mexico, had stopped at the river Grijalva in Yucatan, where he had a battle with the Indians, conquered them, and among the presents they sent him were twenty women slaves. Among these was one whose name will be handed down to future generations, as long as the story of the conquest of Mexico by Cortes is told. She was the daughter of one of the caziques, the Aztec name for the governor of a province or state. Her mother had married, after the death of her first husband, another cazique, by whom she had a son.

Influenced by the wishes of her second husband, who desired to have for his son the property and power this girl would inherit, she was prevailed upon to allow him to give away her daughter to some one belonging to another tribe. This being done, the unnatural mother deceived her friends and relatives with the story that she had died.

The person to whom she had been given sold her to the Tobascans, a tribe living in Yucatan. Here she lived as a slave for many years, and thus happened to be one of the twenty given to Cortes. As she was finely formed, and in all respects a handsome woman, Cortes immediately took her to himself, and she afterwards proved of the greatest service to him as an interpreter. He had her baptised and named Marina, and it is no exaggeration to say that had she not been faithful and loyal to him he would never have been able to conquer the Aztecs. When Cortes landed at the Island of Cozumel, he found a Spaniard by the name of Aquilar, who had been shipwrecked eight years before, and, having lived with the Indians during all that time, had acquired the Tobascan language.

By means of these two persons Cortes was provided with a perfect means of communication with the people from the moment he landed in Mexico ; for he could speak to Aquilar in Spanish, he in Tobascan to Marina, and she to the Aztecs in their own language, which was her native tongue. She proved so apt a scholar that in a remarkably short time she had so far mastered the Spanish language, that Aquilar's services were dispensed with.

Cortes arrived in Mexico on " Holy Thursday," 1519, and met with a friendly reception from the Indians.

In a few days he was waited upon by Tuetile, the general in command of the troops of the Emperor Montezuma, accompanied by Pilpato, the governor of the province in which he had landed. They were attended by a large retinue of officers, and numerous slaves. Cortes was informed of their coming, and met them with all the pomp at his command. They approached him with great ceremony, their salutation being made by one advancing holding and swinging a golden dish filled with burning incense, and at the same time placing upon the censer small straws the ends of which had been dipped in his own blood. This was the customary salutation when meeting an equal. When meeting a superior, the right hand was carried to the ground and then to the head, signifying, " My head is upon the ground before you." Just behind this censer-bearer came the general and governor, who, through Marina, asked Cortes where he came from, and for what purpose he visited their coast ? Cortes replied that he came as an ambassador from

Don Carlos, the great monarch of the East, and asked to see their sovereign.

At the command of the general, thirty Indians came forward loaded with provisions, fine cloth, beautiful feathers of various colors, and a large box containing many pieces of curiously wrought gold, and laid them upon palm leaves which had been spread before Cortes. Then the general, addressing Cortes, said: "I pray you to accept these small presents from two slaves of King Montezuma, who have had orders to entertain such strangers as should come upon his coast; but you must immediately prosecute your voyage, it being no easy matter to speak to the King; and I am doing you no small service in thus undeceiving you, before experience makes you sensible of the difficulty of your pretensions."

The general had not doubted that his order, that the Spaniards immediately leave the country, would be obeyed at once, and was greatly alarmed when Cortes replied, that "Kings always received ambassadors, and he should not leave the country until he had seen his King, Montezuma."

Tuetile and the governor were so surprised at this speech, that for a few moments they remained silent; but they finally informed Cortes that they would send to their monarch for his answer.

Cortes, to impress his visitors with his power and importance, marshalled all his force, men, cannon, and horses, upon the beach, placing the gayest caparisons upon the horses, firing his cannon, and sending the balls flying through the limbs of the trees upon the shore, in order that the general and the governor might see what havoc they could make.

These officers had artists with them who were so skilled in painting as to be able to accurately represent upon cotton cloth everything they saw. They could draw and paint whatever could be thus represented, and by hieroglyphics, signs, and figures describe the whole scene so as to make it fully intelligible. It was afterwards ascertained that they had books written in this way, thus preserving and passing down to future generations the learning and history of the previous age.

When Cortes saw what these painters were doing, he made every display possible, and they accurately represented it upon their canvas, with pictures, hieroglyphics, signs, and figures.

This proves conclusively that the Indians living in Mexico had advanced so far in civilization as to have an intelligent system of chirography. That the Spaniards did not understand it, and could not read it, proves nothing against that fact. Had their descriptions been made in the characters of our present system of stenography, the Spaniards would have thought it a mere conglomeration of unintelligible hieroglyphics, although it is as accurate and intelligible as any other system of writing.

After this display of his resources, Cortes gave a banquet to the Indian officers, and during the conversation ordered one of the pieces of gold that was among the presents to be brought to him, and, showing it to the general, asked if his King had much of that metal. Receiving an affirmative answer, he said, " Let him send it to me, for I and my companions have a complaint, a disease of the heart, which this metal will cure." The Indians have found to their sorrow that this " complaint " was not confined to Cortes and his companions, but is quite universal among white men.

On the departure of the officers, Cortes sent some presents to their King. They returned in seven days with one hundred slaves loaded with presents, which, after the proper ceremony of salutation, were placed upon palm leaves before Cortes, as upon the former occasion. " There were various sorts of cotton robes, well wove, and so fine that they could not be known from silk, but for the feelings ; a quantity of plumes and other curiosities made of feathers, whose beautiful and natural variety of colors the Indian artists knew how to mix and dispose of with so much skill that, without making use of artificial colors or of the pencil, they could draw pictures, and would undertake to imitate nature."

" They next produced a great number of arms, bows and arrows, and targets made of extraordinary woods; also two very large plates of a circular form, the one of gold, which by its embossing represented the sun ; the other of silver, representing the moon ; and lastly a considerable quantity of jewels, pieces of gold, and precious stones; collars of gold, rings, pendants, and other ornaments of great weight, in the shape of birds and beasts, so curiously wrought that, notwithstanding the great value of the metal, the workmanship seemed to exceed it."

When these presents had been laid upon the palm leaves, the general, accompanied by the governor and some other officers, advanced, and turning to Cortes said : " The great Emperor Montezuma has sent you these things in return for your presents, and to show how much he values your King's friendship ; but it is not convenient, nor is it possible at this time, according to the present state of affairs, to grant the permission you ask of passing forward to his Court."

When he had finished speaking, Cortes replied :

" The principal motive my King has in offering his friendship to Montezuma is the obligation Christian princes are under to oppose the errors of idolatry, and the desire he has to instruct the Mexican King in the knowledge of the truth, and under no circumstances shall I leave, until I have seen the country and its King."

This reply angered the Indian general, and turning unceremoniously and sharply toward Cortes, said, " Hitherto the King has treated you courteously and as a guest, but if you continue obstinate, it will be your own fault if you find yourself treated as an enemy."

He exhibited great anger, and as soon as he had finished speaking abruptly turned his back upon Cortes and haughtily walked away, followed by the governor and all his attendants.

Cortes did not like this unpleasant termination of the interview, and immediately prepared himself for defence. The next morning he was surprised to find that the Indians, who had been encamped around

him in great numbers and from whom he had purchased supplies, had disappeared; not a single one
was to be found, and this he at once construed as an
indication of trouble.

It is evident at a glance that the Indians with
whom we are now dealing were far more advanced
in civilization than any we have yet spoken of. We
find them versed in the art of painting and mechanics,
and adepts in the art of diplomacy. We find them
also possessed of a system of chirography which
enabled them to write books and to pass their history
down from generation to generation, in the same
manner as the people inhabiting Europe had done
until about eighty-four years previous, when the art
of printing came into use.

The magnificent presents given by Montezuma
dazzled the eyes of Cortes and his followers, and had
a directly opposite effect from that intended and
hoped for by the giver. Instead of changing his
purpose, Cortes became more than ever desirous to
proceed into the country. The presents had filled
his heart and that of his companions with the wildest emotions, and excited their avarice beyond control. There was not enough gold yet received to
heal the "complaint" of even one of the invaders,
and there were several hundred who were suffering
from the malady.

Shortly after the messengers of Montezuma left him
in anger to report to their sovereign, Cortes received
a message from the cazique of Cempoala (a province
on the Gulf of Mexico about forty miles north of

his present location), offering him a permanent residence in his province, which offer he accepted. He afterwards moved to that province and founded a town, calling it Vera Cruz, a name it still bears.

It was at this place that Cortés discovered a conspiracy forming against him among his own soldiers. He put two of the ringleaders to death, and then resolved to burn his ships, and thus make brave soldiers of his men by destroying any hope they might entertain of returning to Spain; reasoning that, having no means of escape, they must fight to conquer or to die. After taking the sails, cordage, etc., from the ships, he gave the order to apply the torch, and the last vestige of hope in the breasts of the disaffected sank to the bottom of the Gulf.

These Indians, although far in advance of their northern brethren in civilization, were worshippers of idols, and had upon their escutcheon the dark stain of sacrificing human beings in their religious ceremonies. This was very repugnant to Cortes, and in a few days he sent a body of troops and hurled the idols from the temples. This greatly incensed the natives, who at once rushed to arms to avenge the insult to their gods. Cortes immediately seized the cazique and all the principal chiefs, and declared that they should be put to death if any harm was done the Spaniards. The threat had the desired effect, and the natives were awed into submission.

While Cortes was at Vera Cruz, the collectors of Montezuma came into the province to collect the tribute. Cortes seized them, and ordered that no tribute should be paid. This greatly pleased the Cempoalans, and made them his fast friends.

The reason why the cazique of Cempoala invited Cortes to his province, and why the people so readily forgave him his great insult to their gods, is found in their belief in a prevailing legend—a legend connected with the mythology of their country, and implicitly believed in by the entire nation, both rulers and people. The people believed it with joy, and the rulers with fear; but like the great majority of Indians, many of the rulers were content to accept what they considered the inevitable, and to submit to it.

Indians as a class are fatalists, and yield without a struggle to what they believe to be the inevitable. The Emperor Montezuma was tainted with this superstition as much as any of his subjects, and the Spaniards owe their success to his belief and the universal belief in this legend.

The legend runs as follows :

In the long ago, Quetzalcoatl (God of the Air) was a divinity who, during his residence on earth, instructed the people in the use of metals, in agriculture, in many of the arts, in astronomy, and in government. During his earthly sojourn, fruits, flowers, and corn grew spontaneously. Cotton grew not only white, but variegated in all the colors of the rainbow. The "God of the Air" made everything beautiful; life was one unalloyed round of pleasure and delight. After a time, the other gods became jealous of the adoration and love the "God of the Air " was receiving from all the people, and joining together, compelled him to abandon the country. On his way to the East, he stopped at the city of Cholula, where a temple was built for him and dedicated to his worship, the massive ruins of which still form one of the most interesting relics of antiquity in Mexico. The other gods were not content with his remaining even in one city, but compelled him to pursue his journey to the eastward. When he reached the Gulf of Mexico, he took leave of his followers, who were from all parts of the country, but promised them that he *or his descendants* would visit them again at some future time; and that when he *or his descendants* should come, they would take possession of the country and govern it in such a manner that the inhabitants would be restored to all the blessings they had enjoyed while he resided among them.

After making this promise, he entered his canoe made of serpents' skins, embarked on the great ocean, and was lost to view in the distant East. He had a white skin, dark hair, and a flowing beard.

The Mexicans waited in confident and happy expectation for the return of their beloved deity, and it was this wonderful legend, so firmly believed in and so deeply cherished, that opened the way for Cortes.

The Spaniards came from the East and had " white skins," " dark hair " and " flowing beards," all the external features which the descendants of the " God of the Air " would naturally possess. Therefore all the people wished to welcome the white strangers, and were willing and prepared to receive them with open arms.

Not so, however, with some of the rulers. On the return of the " God of the Air," all kings and rulers would be overthrown, and he alone would rule in peace and plenty. The rulers therefore feared and dreaded his coming, as it would sound the death-knell of their power. Many of the caziques, however, were so influenced by this belief, that they thought it foolish and worse than useless to fight against the men with the "white skin," as they would surely triumph in the end, and then the " God of the Air " would punish severely all those who had opposed his children.

It was this belief that prompted the cazique of Cempoala to invite Cortes to his province, and his people to forgive his insult to their gods and become his fast friends.

On the fifteenth day of August, 1519, Cortes started on his march towards the City of Mexico, the residence of the great King of whom he had heard so much, and from whom he had received such magnificent presents. His force consisted of four hundred Spaniards, thirteen hundred Cempoalan warriors, and one thousand carriers to draw his cannon, carry his baggage, etc.

The first opposition he met was from the Tlascalans, a tribe occupying a province that had ever maintained its independence of the Aztec monarch. Cortes sent messengers to the rulers of Tlascala, asking permission to pass through their country on his way to the City of Mexico.

A council was at once convened, at which the question was discussed. Some of the leading men argued that the "white skins" must surely be the descendants of the "God of the Air," and should be allowed to pass unmolested, as they desired. Others, however, maintained that whether they were such descendants or not, they should be opposed and driven from the country, if possible, as all rulers would be hurled from power if the "white skins" were successful. A compromise was finally reached between these opposing factions, by which it was determined that their army should fall upon the Spaniards and crush them if possible; and if they should be victorious, it would prove that the "pale faces" were not gods, or the descendants of the "God of the Air," and if the "white skins" should gain a victory, the council could act afterwards. They detained the couriers Cortes had sent, so that their army could reach him before he could know the result of their mission. The Indians poured upon Cortes in almost countless numbers, but they found him fully prepared. They had never been confronted with fire-arms before, and therefore advanced in dense columns, expecting to crush Cortes with the force of mere numerical strength ; but, at the first discharge of the cannon and musketry, they were mown down by hundreds. They were utterly dumfounded by the shock and fearful slaughter, but rallied and made charge after charge, until the fate

of the Spaniards trembled in the balance.   Cortes
saw his men weakening, but by wonderful personal
daring encouraged and rallied them, until finally the
cannon and musketry were victorious, and the Indians retreated.

The common warriors were almost naked, but the
caziques and chiefs were clothed in quilted cotton
armor, two inches thick, fitting closely to their entire
bodies.   Over this the wealthier ones wore cuirasses
of gold or silver plate.   Their legs were covered
with leather boots trimmed with gold.   Some of
them had a beautiful mantle decorated with feathers,
and upon their heads a cap of wood or leather
representing the head of some wild animal, somewhat similar to that worn by the Thlinkeets, which
I have heretofore described.   From the top of this
cap floated a beautiful plume made of richly variegated feathers, indicating by its form and color the
rank and family of the wearer.

This cotton armor would doubtless have been
serviceable against arrows and lances, but it formed
no defence against cannon-balls, and little if any
against the bullets of the musketry.   It was afterwards adopted by the Spaniards, as being equal to
their own against arrows and spears, and having the
great advantage of being much lighter.

After this terrible defeat, and a slaughter such as
they had never before known, the Tlascalans held
another council, into the deliberations of which they
called their priests.   The priests maintained that
the strangers were not gods, but were children of

the sun, and derived their strength from it ; and that if they were attacked in the night, when there was no sun to help them, they could be easily vanquished.

The party who were still of the belief that the " white skins " were the descendants of the " God of the Air," pointed to the fearful slaughter caused by so few against so many, and maintained that none other than children of a God could make the thunder and lightning fight for them. They could compare the roar and flash of the artillery to nothing but thunder and lightning. This party still asserted that it was worse than useless to fight against destiny, and advised peace ; but the oracles, as delivered through the priests, had the most influence upon the minds of the councillors, and the general of the army was ordered to make a night attack.

Selecting a bright moonlight night, he rushed his army upon the camp of the strangers with an impetuosity almost overpowering. It was in this attack that an Indian is said to have severed the head of one of the horses completely from its body with one blow of a peculiar sword of Indian manufacture. But Cortes was again prepared, and the Indians met with as signal a defeat as that which had attended them under the full glare of the sun.

Another council was held, and it was therein agreed, with practical unanimity, that the strangers must be the descendants of the " God of the Air," and it was further decided to make peace with them upon the best terms obtainable. A small body of

Indians dressed in white, to indicate that their mission was one of peace, were sent to the Spanish camp
and were admitted. They brought some provisions
and a few presents, and said they were sent by the
Tlascalan general to say that he was weary of the
war and desired peace; and that, if agreeable, he
would come himself in a few days and complete
the arrangements. After a day or two, some of
these Indians left the camp, while about fifty
remained. Cortes suspected that they were spies,
and ordered *their hands cut off*, and in this maimed
and helpless condition sent them away with a message to their general that the Tlascalans might come
by day or night, and they would find the Spaniards
ready for them. The return of these men to their
countrymen, in this mutilated condition, did much
toward dispelling the belief that the strangers were
the descendants of the good "God of the Air."
They could not account for such cruelty.

We can never know whether Cortes had good
ground for his suspicions, but knowing as we now do
the condition of the Indians, and that they had already determined to make peace with the strangers
prior to sending these men to Cortes' camp, the
probabilities are all against their being spies; and it
seems likely that Cortes indulged in this heartless
barbarity more to impress the Indians, than from
fear of any actual damage that these Indians might
do him by spying upon his camp. The mere fact of
his letting them go, knowing that they could tell all

they had seen as well without hands as with, seems conclusive proof that his act was one of mere wanton cruelty, like the similar one of De Soto. In either case, putting the victims to death would have shown far less of barbarity and cruelty.

15

CHAPTER XVI.

ON the second day following the events narrated
in the last chapter, the Tlascalan general came
to the camp, with a numerous train of attendants. The Spaniards gazed admiringly upon this
valiant chief as he advanced with firm and fearless
tread, as if coming to bid defiance rather than to sue
for peace. He was a large man, with a fine physique,
and about thirty-five years of age. When he came
into the presence of Cortes, he saluted by touching
the ground with his hand and carrying it to his head
(the salute to a superior), while the sweet incense of
aromatic gums arose in clouds from the censers carried by his slaves.

The salutations ended, he made a speech to Cortes
(interpreted by Marina), in which he said: " I considered the white men enemies, for they came with
the Cempoalans, who are the allies and vassals of
King Montezuma. I love my country, and wish to
preserve the independence she has maintained through
her long wars with the Aztecs. I have been beaten.
You may be the strangers who, it has been so long
predicted, would come from the East, to take possession of the country. I hope you will use your

victory with moderation, and not trample upon the liberties of my country. I come now in the name of my nation to tender its obedience, assuring you that you will find my countrymen as faithful in peace as they have been brave in war." `

Cortes replied: "I am willing to bury in oblivion your past bad conduct in fighting me, and will receive the Tlascalans as vassals to the Emperor, my master. If you prove true, I will remain your friend: if false, I will wreak speedy vengeance upon you."

At the conclusion of the speeches, the general withdrew with as much ceremony as he had approached.

Before the Tlascalans had left the camp, an embassy arrived from King Montezuma. Couriers had kept him thoroughly posted in regard to the doings of the Spaniards, and he knew how terribly the Tlascalans had been slaughtered by the little band of white men. These things had put him in mortal fear, for he was a firm believer in the legend, and thought he saw in the "white skin, black hair, and flowing beards" of the Spaniards the "men of destiny" who were to take possession of his sceptre.

In his alarm he had sent a new embassy to the Spanish camp. It consisted of five great nobles, with two hundred slaves. They carried a present of three thousand ounces of gold in grains and some curiously manufactured articles in gold, besides several hundred mantles and dresses of cotton, finely embroidered, and much beautiful feather work.

After the presentation of the presents, one of the

nobles stepped forward and, turning to Cortes, said :
" We have come to present you with these few gifts,
and to offer you the congratulations of King Montezuma, upon the victories you have won. He also
instructed us to say, that it was still out of his power
to receive you at his capital, as the people are so
unruly that your safety would be placed in jeopardy."
Cortes replied : " I have orders from the great Emperor of the East to visit the capital of your sovereign, and communicate with him face to face,
and under no circumstances can his orders be
disobeyed."

The ambassadors seeing the determination of
Cortes, and that their arguments had no weight with
him, offered a tribute to the Spanish sovereign, if
Cortes would relinquish his intended visit to the
capital.

This offer of a tribute at once revealed fear upon
the part of Montezuma, which Cortes was not slow
to perceive, and he reiterated that by reason of the
commands of his sovereign he would be obliged to
disregard the wishes of Montezuma. At the same
time he expressed the most profound respect for the
Aztec sovereign, and said that although he had not
the means at the present time to requite his munificence, he hoped and trusted he would have the opportunity at some future day to repay him with
" good works."

We will see hereafter with what " good works " he
repaid him.

Several of the ambassadors returned at once to the

City of Mexico to inform their sovereign of the
result of their mission, while others remained with
Cortes. After a few days he marched into the City
of Tlascala, about eighteen miles distant.

His line of march led through a hilly region, ex-
hibiting in every arable patch of ground evidences
of laborious cultivation. Over one of the ravines
was an arched stone bridge on which Cortes crossed
with all his army. They passed quite a number of
small towns, and as they approached the city were
met by an immense throng of men, women, and children, with bunches and wreathes of roses and various
other beautiful flowers, which they presented to the
Spaniards. Priests in their white robes mingled with
the crowd, sending up volumes of incense from their
burning censers. The crowd was so great that it
was difficult for the native police to clear and keep
open a passage-way for the white army. The houses
were festooned with flowers, and arches of evergreen
boughs, intertwined with roses and honeysuckles,
were built over the streets. The procession moved
through the principal streets, and came to a halt in
front of the mansion of the most aged of the rulers
of the country, whose son was the general of the
Army. This ruler was nearly blind, and to satisfy
his curiosity in regard to the wonderful white men,
passed his hand over the face and person of Cortes.
He then led the way to a spacious hall in the mansion, where he had had a banquet prepared for the
Spaniards, and they all partook of it. After the
feast they were shown to their quarters in build-

ings and grounds surrounding one of the large temples.

And these were Indians, and Cortes was in an Indian city, where no white man had ever set his foot before ; Indians who had never learned anything of architecture, government, or civility, except through the development of their own brain.

Did not their diplomacy, speeches, giving of flowers, festooning of the houses, and building of evergreen and floral arches over the streets, denote civilization and even high culture?

While in this city, Cortes wrote a letter to the Spanish Emperor, in which he compares Tlascala with Granada. He said: " It is larger, stronger, and more populous than the Moorish capital, and quite as well built. The better class of houses are built of stone and lime, others of brick dried in the sun. The doors and windows are made of mats, with pieces of copper or something which by its tinkling sound will give notice of any one's entrance. Thirty thousand people are often gathered together upon the plazas upon fair- or market-days, which occur every fifth day. They excel in pottery, and the inhabitants from the surrounding country bring in their wares and provisions to sell or exchange. They also have barber-shops and baths, both of vapor and hot water, and the inhabitants make great use of them."

This indicates a very decided advance in civilization.

The city was divided into four distinct quarters,

separated by high stone walls. A swift running stream coursed through it, which as it entered furnished water for the inhabitants, and as it left was utilized as a sewer for the city. The Tlascalan led a life of temperance and toil, earned his bread by the sweat of his brow, and was patriotic and independent.

For several days the Spaniards were entertained at the hospitable boards of the four great rulers, and during this time the rulers presented Cortes with three or four hundred maidens, among whom were several daughters of the caziques. His religious scruples would not allow him to accept them until they were baptised, so a great ceremony was held, and each maiden was formally baptised, and given a new name. The ceremony ended, Cortes assigned the daughters of the caziques to his officers, and the remainder of the maidens he distributed among his Christian soldiery.

While still in this city, Montezuma sent another embassy to Cortes, this time changing his tone entirely, inviting him to his capital, and asking him to take the route through the friendly city of Cholula, where by his royal orders arrangements would be made for his reception.

The Tlascalans tried to dissuade him from going to the City of Mexico, or putting any trust in Montezuma, saying that his armies spread over every part of the country, and that in his capital, on account of its insular position, the Spaniards could easily be entrapped. They said : "Trust not his fair words,

his courtesies and his gifts, his professions are false."
This affords another illustration of the true friendship of Indians for those whom they consider friends.

After listening quietly to all they had to say,
Cortes replied: "I know from what I have heard
that Montezuma is a great King, and has large armies,
but he is not invincible, as you well know, for you
yourselves have beaten him in many battles, and have
maintained your own independence of him for many
years. I have commands from my sovereign to
proceed to the capital, and my sovereign is so much
greater and so much more powerful than Montezuma,
that his commands cannot be disobeyed, and I know
I can withstand all the armies Montezuma can send
against me."

He also very adroitly insinuated that if they would
join their army with his they would reap great benefit, for in that way they would see Montezuma hum-
bled, and would make their independence of him
doubly sure.

This thought pleased the Tlascalans, and thousands
of their warriors volunteered to accompany him, many
more than he thought best to take. He selected six
thousand of their best fighting and best-armed men,
and on the appointed day started.

Bernald Diaz, who was with Cortes, says: "On
the way we found rich products of various climes
growing side by side, fields of fine large maize, the
juicy aloe, the pepper, and large plantations of the
cactus, on which the cochineal feed. We did not see
a rood of arable land that was not under cultivation.

In many places the soil was irrigated by numerous streams and artificial canals."

This description is given by one of the first white men who ever saw that country, and where in the civilized world can be found a better system of agriculture, or more thorough farming, than existed among the Indians of Mexico?

When Cortes arrived at Cholula he camped just outside the city, where he was met by the caziques. The Cholulans objected to having their enemies, the Tlascalans, enter the city, and Cortes, appreciating their objection, had them remain outside, while he and his Spaniards entered, attended only by enough Cempoalans to draw the cannon and carry the baggage.

The Tlascalans gave him many cautions about the Cholulans, telling him that he could not trust them, and earnestly advising him to be on the constant lookout for them, as they were treacherous and cunning.

The reception given Cortes at Cholula was similar to that at Tlascala—crowds, flowers, festooned buildings, evergreen arches, etc.

The Spaniards were surprised to find the Cholulans a superior-looking people to any they had yet seen. They were better dressed, the richer classes wearing fine embroidered mantles resembling the graceful Moorish cloak. The people were more quiet and orderly, and seemed to be under better discipline and government. The Spaniards were astonished at the cleanliness of the city, and the great width and regularity of the streets, which had evidently been laid

out on a well-settled plan; also with the size and
solidity of the houses, and the number and size of
the temples. Their dimensions can be imagined from
the fact that the Spaniards, numbering about four
hundred, with their Cempoalan attendants, numbering about one thousand, as well as the four hundred
maidens, were all quartered in the court of one of
them.

They were visited by all the great nobles, who
provided most bountifully for their table, and expressed so much solicitude for their welfare and
comfort that it completely disarmed them of all
suspicions of treachery.

After a few days of this rest and feasting, some messengers arrived from Montezuma and told Cortes that
his approach to the City of Mexico was causing much
disquietude, and after conferring with the ambassadors of Montezuma who had remained in Cortes' camp,
withdrew, taking one of the ambassadors with them.

After this, everything was changed. The nobles
ceased to visit the Spaniards, and when invited would
excuse themselves on the ground of illness. Cortes
knew that this boded no good, and was exceedingly
troubled. Some of the Cempoalans in their walks
through the city had seen some of the streets barri-
caded, and large piles of stones on the flat roofs of
some of the houses; others had discovered holes dug
across the street in places, and covered so as to avoid
detection, and that these holes had upright stakes
planted in the bottom of them; others had seen great
numbers of women and children leaving the city.

All these reports confirmed Cortes in the belief that some hostile scheme was on foot.

Marina was a most faithful friend of Cortes, and she now proved his guardian angel. During their stay at Cholula, a wife of one of the caziques had become much interested in her, often inviting her to visit at her home, which she did. On one occasion the wife intimated to her that she had better leave the Spaniards and come to her house. Marina had a fine, bright mind, and at once surmised that something was going to happen, so in order to gain the secret, she pretended she was heartily tired of being held a prisoner among the Spaniards, and would rejoice in their destruction. She was so adroit and seemed so sincere in what she said as to completely deceive the woman and disarm her of all suspicion, so that she unfolded to Marina the entire plan.

She said that Montezuma had sent rich presents to the caziques, her husband among the rest, to get them to destroy the Spaniards. They were to be assaulted as they marched out of the city, and a great many things had been done to prevent their marching in any order or haste. Montezuma had already sent a force of twenty thousand men, who were now encamped not far from the city, to assist in the attack, and she thought the " pale faces " would all be killed, as they would be taken unawares.

As soon as possible Marina informed Cortes of all she had learned. Cortes then bribed two priests, with some of the rich presents Montezuma had sent him, to tell him all the details of the plot, which they did. He then sent word to the caziques that he should leave the city on the morning of the next day.

In the morning he started, and soon saw several thousand men standing in the streets and open places, all armed. He at once opened fire upon them with great slaughter, piling the ground with the slain. They thought Cortes would suppose the warriors had been gathered for an honorary escort to him, and this sudden and unexpected attack and fearful slaughter threw them into the wildest disorder and confusion, and, at a preconcerted signal, the six thousand Tlascalans, ever the hated enemies of the Cholulans, poured upon the flying warriors with terrible fury. So great was the dismay and terror caused by this sudden, unexpected, and fearful discharge of cannon and musketry, something their ears had never heard nor their eyes seen, that it was impossible to rally them, and the Tlascalans had a fine opportunity to wreak vengeance upon their old and hated foes.

The flying Cholulans, rushing into the camp in such fearful disorder and fright, carried dismay to Montezuma's forces, and soon all were flying before the victorious army of Cortes.

The Spaniards and Tlascalans then ransacked and pillaged the city. Order was finally established, by prevailing upon some of the Cholulan caziques to return, and through them the people. There were about five thousand Cholulan warriors slain.

This was the first time the natives had felt the white man's vengeance. They had met him in battle and been conquered, but there the slaughter had ended. Here terrible vengeance had been wreaked upon them for daring to conspire against the Spaniards. They had been slaughtered by thousands, and their city pillaged and robbed of everything of value. No wonder the natives believed the white men "gods," little thinking that it was only powder and ball that gave them this superior power.

This affair created fearful consternation throughout the entire empire. The Indians were now convinced that the men with the " white skin " were not only invincible in arms, but that they possessed an attribute of the gods—the foreknowledge of events. It was a mystery to them how Cortes could have known of the conspiracy to destroy him, before a single arrow had been shot or the slightest intimation given of such an intention. The result was that many caziques immediately sent envoys to the Spanish camp, tendering their allegiance and suing for favor by rich presents of gold and slaves.

Montezuma trembled upon his throne. He was amazed, bewildered. His mind turned gloomily to the reference to the legend made in the speech at his accession. This speech has been literally translated, and the allusion to the legend was as follows:

" Perhaps you are dismayed at the prospect of the terrible calamities that are one day to overwhelm us ; calamities foreseen and foretold, though not felt by

our forefathers; when the destruction and desolation
of the Empire shall come; when all shall be plunged
into darkness; when the hour shall arrive in which
they shall make us slaves throughout the land, and
we shall be condemned to the lowest and most
degrading offices."

This is an exact translation from their records. It
shows us what a strong hold that legend had taken
upon the minds and hearts of the people of that
empire. They firmly believed it, and that was the
reason why some of the caziques thought it worse
than useless to contend against the "white skins,"
for if not successful (which they fully believed they
would not be), they would be terribly punished for
having done so.

Montezuma feared the time had come for the ful-
filment of this prophecy. Everything looked like
it. His courage and prowess, that had enabled him
to conquer province after province and add them to
his empire, now forsook him entirely. He was beginning to think the white strangers invincible, as
everything seemed to indicate that they were the
agents of destruction referred to in the ancient
prophecy. He again sent envoys to Cortes, bearing,
as before, rich presents of gold plate and ornaments
of gold, among which were beautifully carved birds
wrought in this precious metal, and many garments
made of the finest and most delicate fabrics. These
were sent, the envoys said, merely to reassure Cortes
of the Emperor's good wishes.

A little more than two weeks after Cortes' arrival

at Cholula, he again started on his march for the
City of Mexico. He found the land under the same
state of cultivation that had existed between Tlascala
and Cholula. Large and luxuriant plantations extended on every side, watered by natural streams or
irrigated by artificial canals. On the mountain passes
were commodious stone buildings which the government had placed here and there, for the accommoda-
tion of travellers and government couriers passing
over these cold and bleak mountains. As they
descended upon the other side, they were surprised
to see a beautiful valley "spread out like a gay
panorama." Stretching far at their feet were large
fields of maize and also of maguey, intermingled with
orchards and blooming gardens. Flowers were even
more abundant in this valley than in the other parts
of the country they had passed, and considerable
attention seemed to have been given to their cultivation and arrangement in beds, with reference to
ornamentation in the blending of colors. The centre of this valley was filled with lakes, their borders
thickly studded with towns and hamlets, and in the
midst of these lakes—" Like some Indian empress
with her coronal of pearls "—stood the fair city, with
her white towers and massive temples, reposing, as
it were, on the bosom of the waters—the far-famed
City of Mexico—the " Venice of the Aztecs." The
hill of Chapultepec, upon which was the summer
residence of the monarch, rose high over the city,
and extended to the shore of the lake.

Such was the beautiful vision that broke upon the

eyes of the Spaniards. They saw in all this the
evidence of a civilization and power far superior to
anything they had yet encountered.

When Montezuma heard that these strange men,
so invincible in war, so impregnable to bribes, had
really crossed the mountains and were in the valley
near his capital, he went into a paroxysm of despair,
shut himself up in his palace, refused food, and
sought relief in prayer. He was now convinced
that these were they whose coming had been foretold.

At last he called a council. His nobles were divided in opinion. Some advised receiving the strangers courteously, as ambassadors of a great sovereign ;
others advised gathering his army at once and fighting to the death.

But Montezuma was completely under the spell of
the ancient prophecy, and with downcast eye, and
dejected mien, said : " Of what avail is resistance
when the gods have declared themselves against us ?
Yet I mourn most for the old and infirm, the women
and the children, too feeble to fight or to fly. For
myself and the brave men around us, we must bare
our breasts to the storm, and meet it as we may."

After the council was dismissed, Montezuma concluded to try once more to conciliate the Spaniards.
He immediately sent another embassy, consisting of
several Aztec nobles, bearing as usual large presents
of gold and robes of beautiful furs and feathers.
This time he offered a large bribe to them if they
would return and not visit his capital. He prom-

ised four loads of gold to the General, and one to each of the captains, with a yearly tribute to their sovereign. Thus effectually had the lofty and naturally courageous spirit of the Indian monarch been subdued by the influence of superstition. His firm belief in the prophecy had taken away all his spirit and courage.

Cortes received the gifts in a courteous manner, but, as might have been expected, replied that it was impossible for him to disobey the commands of his sovereign, who had ordered him to visit the capital of the renowned Aztec monarch and confer with him face to face. He also informed the ambassadors that he came in the spirit of peace, and that Montezuma would be convinced of that fact by his actions.

16

CHAPTER XVII.

THE Spaniards had remained two days at a town containing many thousand inhabitants, and upon their departure the cazique gave them gold to the amount of three thousand "castellanos." After leaving this place, they passed through large plantations of maize and maguey, which latter may be called the Aztec vineyards.

Cortes next stopped at a town built over the water. The canals which intersected the city in lieu of streets were full of boats loaded with provisions, various kinds of merchandise, etc., going to and fro. The Spaniards were struck with the style and commodious structure of the houses, built chiefly of stone, and having the general appearance of wealth and luxury. The sentries, fearful of treachery, shot down fifteen or twenty Indians the first night.

The next morning the cazique of Texcuco, who was the next in rank to Montezuma, came to visit Cortes. He was brought in a palanquin, richly decorated with plates of gold and precious stones and having a canopy of green plumes supported by curiously wrought pillars, borne upon the shoulders of his carriers. He was also accompanied by a large number of nobles and attendants. When he approached Cortes, he descended from his palanquin, and his slaves swept the ground before him as he advanced. He was a young man, about twenty-five years of age, of fine presence, erect and stately in his deportment. After making the usual salutation to persons of high rank, he informed Cortes that he came as the representative of Montezuma to bid the Spaniards welcome to the capital. He then presented Cortes with three pearls of uncommon size and lustre. Cortes presented him with a chain of cut glass, and assured him of his friendly intentions. The Indian prince then took his departure. The Spaniards were impressed with his state and bearing. The nearer they came to the throne the more superior were the men they met.

After the prince had departed, Cortes resumed his march. His army passed through orchards filled with rich and strange fruits, and through cultivated fields irrigated by canals bringing water from a neighboring lake. The whole country showed a careful and economical husbandry.

A causeway four or five miles in length, ten or twelve feet in width in its narrowest part, and wide enough for eight horsemen to ride abreast, was the next object of interest. It was a solid structure of stone and lime, running directly through the lake, a most remarkable piece of work. Here they saw floating gardens, that looked like islands of flowers and vegetables moving over the waters. All around the margin of the lake, at times extending quite a distance into and over the water, were little

towns and villages, half concealed by the foliage.
The Spaniards were amazed at the scene. They
could compare it to nothing they had ever known,
for it seemed more like fairy-land, than anything
in real life.

Midway across the lake was a town, composed
of more beautiful houses than any they had yet
seen. Here Cortes halted for refreshments. Proceeding on his journey, he came to a place called
Iztapalapan, containing some twelve or fifteen
thousand houses, the residence of a brother of
King Montezuma, and the ruler of the place. He,
after giving Cortes a present of gold and other
articles, invited him with his men to a banquet
served in one of the great halls of his palace.
Cortes, writing to the King of Spain, says of this
place: "The architecture is excellent, and I do
not hesitate to say that some of the buildings are
equal to the best in Spain. They are of stone,
and the spacious apartments have roofs of odorous
cedar wood, and the walls are hung with tapestry
of fine cottons with brilliant colorings."

"The pride of Iztapalapan," on which its lord
had freely lavished his care and revenues, was its
beautiful gardens. They covered an immense tract
of land ; were laid out in regular squares, and the
paths intersecting them were bordered with trel-
lises, supporting creepers and aromatic shrubs that
filled the air with their perfumes. The gardens
were stocked with fruit-trees imported from distant places, and with the gaudy family of flowers

which belong to the Mexican flora, *scientifically
arranged*, and growing luxuriantly in the equable
temperature of the table-land. The natural dry-
ness of the atmosphere was counteracted by means
of aqueducts and canals, which carried water into
all parts of the grounds.

In one quarter was an aviary filled with numerous
kinds of birds, remarkable in this region for bril-
liancy of plumage. The gardens were intersected
by a canal communicating with the lake Texcuco,
and of sufficient size for barges to enter from the
latter. But the most elaborate piece of work was
a huge reservoir of stone, filled to a considerable
height with water well supplied with different
kinds of fish. This reservoir was four thousand
eight hundred feet in circumference, and was surrounded by a walk, made also of stone, wide
enough for four persons to walk abreast. The
sides were curiously sculptured, having a flight of
steps leading to the water below. Many fountains
added their beauty to the scene.

Such are the accounts of these beautiful gardens,
at a period when similar horticulture was unknown
in Europe. We cannot doubt their existence, as
they were matters of such notoriety at the time, and
are so thoroughly attested.

Cortes remained in this town over night. His
force consisted of about seven thousand, of whom
less than four hundred were Spaniards. His cavalry
amounted to fifteen horses. Another causeway
connected the town of Iztapalapan with the City of

Mexico. This was wide enough for ten horsemen to ride abreast. It was solidly built of stone, laid in cement, and astonished the Spaniards with its mechanical construction, and geometrical precision. At the distance of one and a half miles from the capital, a solid work of stone, twelve feet high, was built directly across the causeway, strengthened by towers at each end, and in the centre was a gateway for the passage of the troops.

Here he was met by a large number of Aztec chiefs, who came to announce the approach of Montezuma. They were richly and gaily dressed. About their necks and upon their arms were collars and bracelets of turquoise mosaic, with which delicate plumage was curiously mingled. Each cazique saluted Cortes with the salutation due a superior, and there were so many of them that the ceremony delayed him more than an hour. This finished, he marched on until he came to a wooden drawbridge which was just in front of the walls of the city. As soon as they had passed the bridge, they saw the glittering retinue of the Emperor coming down the wide street of the city.

Montezuma came in a palanquin blazing with burnished gold, preceded by three nobles bearing golden wands. Over the palanquin was a canopy of gaudy featherwork, interspersed with jewels and fringed with silver. It was borne upon the shoulders of nobles of high rank, and the canopy was also carried by nobles. The nobles bearing the palanquin and canopy were all barefooted, and walked with a slow and measured tread, and with eyes bent upon the ground. When within a convenient distance, Montezuma alighted and came forward, leaning upon the arms of the chiefs of Iztapalapan and Texcuco, his brother and nephew, both of whom had already been introduced to Cortes.

As the monarch advanced, the canopy was carried over his head, and attendants placed cotton tapestry before him, so that his imperial feet should not touch the ground. His subjects of high degree, who lined the sides of the causeway, stood with heads bowed low, and their eyes resting on the ground. Those of low degree prostrated themselves before him.

" Montezuma wore the girdle and ample square cloak of his nation. It was made of the finest cotton, with the embroidered ends gathered in a knot around his neck. His feet were defended by sandals having soles of gold, and the leather thongs that bound them to his ankles were embossed with the same metal. Both the cloak and sandals were decorated with pearls and precious stones, among which the emerald and the chalchivitl (a green stone of higher estimation than any other among the Aztecs) were conspicuous. On his head he wore a cap of plumes of the royal green which floated down his back, the badge of military rather than regal rank. He was at this time about forty years of age, was tall and thin, but well proportioned. His hair, which was black and straight, was not very long. His beard was thin, and his complexion somewhat paler than was often seen among his copper-colored race. His features, though serious in their expres-

sion, did not wear the look of melancholy or dejection.
He moved with dignity, and his whole demeanor,
tempered by an expression of benignity, was worthy
of a great prince.

"When he approached, Cortes dismounted, and,
attended by a few of his principal officers, advanced
to meet him. It was a strange sight to both, but
particularly to the Aztec Emperor, who saw a "white
face" for the first time, and in that white face saw
the strange being whose history seemed to be so
mysteriously connected with his own; the predicted
one of his oracles, whose achievements proclaimed
him something more than human.

"But whatever the monarch's feelings may have
been, he so far suppressed them as to receive his
guest with princely courtesy, and to graciously welcome him to his capital. Cortes responded with the
most profound expressions of respect, and made
ample acknowledgments for the substantial proofs
which the Emperor had given the Spaniards of his
munificence. He then hung around Montezuma's
neck a sparkling chain of colored crystals, accom-
panying this act with a movement as if to embrace
him, when he was restrained by two of the Aztec
nobles, who were shocked at the menaced profana-
tion of the sacred person of their monarch.

"After the civilities were finished, Montezuma
instructed his brother to conduct the Spaniards to
their quarters in the city, and entering his palanquin
was borne off amid prostrate crowds, in the same
stately manner in which he had come."

The Spaniards soon followed, and with music and flying colors marched to the quarters prepared for them in the southern quarter of the great capital of Mexico, which they had so longed to see and enter.

It is strange how historians differ in their accounts of newly discovered nations.

Lord Macaulay says that, " The victories of Cortes had been gained over savages who had no letters, who were ignorant of the use of metals, who had not broken in a single animal to labor, who wielded no better weapons than those that could be made out of sticks, flints, and fish bones, and who regarded a horse-soldier as a monster, half man and half beast."

Other historians, and the facts, differ widely from this estimate.

Prior to the arrival of Cortes, no white man had ever been among these people. We therefore have no description of the natives of this country, prior to that written by the men who accompanied him. That they did not exaggerate, is proven by the fact that they are corroborated by other writers of the same century, and by the few ancient manuscripts, hieroglyphics, and picture-writings of the natives, which fortunately escaped the general destruction and which have been interpreted by those whose only ambition has been to get at the truth.

All these historians contradict Lord Macaulay, and agree in saying that the Mexican Indians were a vast people ; " that they were not like the Indians of the islands, living in huts, but lived in substantial stone houses, and formed a mighty kingdom, mighty at least in appearance, with dependant states that paid tribute to King Montezuma; that these Indians were possessed of a fierce and pertinacious bravery ; that their weapons were bows and arrows, a formidable sword, and javelins tipped with copper, and that they would not have been contemptible anywhere in a previous age ; that they were expert marksmen—it not being an unusual thing for archers to assemble together and throw an ear of maize into the air, at which they immediately shot with such quickness and dexterity, that before it reached the ground it would be struck with many arrows." Horses were unknown to the Mexican Indians and it was no wonder they looked upon the horse-soldiers of Cortes as monsters.

That does not show (as Lord Macaulay seemed to think) that the Mexican Indians were very far from being civilized. The old Romans were quite advanced in civilization, yet their legions were overcome by fear, and thrown into the greatest confusion, by the strange appearance of the elephants in their first engagement with Pyrrhus.

The descriptions given of the houses, cultivation of lands, and the customs of the native Indians whom Cortes met, showed that they were far advanced in civilization. It is indeed a question whether they were not further advanced than their conquerors. True, they were idolators, and the black stain of human sacrifice was upon their hands ; a thing to us most abhorrent, but with them robbed to a great extent of its sting by the prevailing superstition "that he who died in battle, or upon the altar of the gods, went directly to heaven." This belief was so prevalent and so firmly rooted in the minds of the people, that many, of their own free will, offered themselves to the priests for sacrifice.

Putting aside this one great blot, we find a nation far advanced in architecture, art, astronomy, chirography, and government ; and these constitute civilization. We have seen what fine architecture the Spaniards found throughout the country, and in this the capital, the residence of their monarch, it was even more beautiful and massive. A palace built by Montezuma's father, and which had stood about fifty years, was appropriated to the Spaniards. When they arrived, the Emperor was there in the courtyard waiting to receive them. He had with him a beautiful vase of flowers, and a massive collar made of gold, equal in workmanship to anything the goldsmiths in Europe could make, and costly shells, which were set in gold and fastened together with heavy links of the same metal ; also eight heavy golden pendants wrought in curious shapes and designs, and of delicate workmanship. Montezuma hung the collar around the neck of Cortes, at the same time making him a present of the palace and its grounds, after which he took his departure.

The building was spacious, one story in height, except in the centre, where it was two. The apartments were of great size, affording accommodations for the whole of Cortes' army. The best apartments were hung with gay draperies, and the floors covered with mats. There were stools or chairs made of wood, elaborately carved, and in most of the apartments were beds made of palm leaves woven into a thick mattress, with coverlets and canopies of cotton.

Montezuma visited them again the next day, and asked many questions about the Spaniards—where they came from, what they came for, etc. Before leaving, he presented Cortes with clothing for every man in his army, including the allies, and also with gold chains and other ornaments in great profusion. He then withdrew, leaving the Spaniards deeply impressed with his munificence and affability, so unlike what they had been led to expect.

Cortes, ostensibly to celebrate the arrival of his army in the City of Mexico, but in reality to let the inhabitants of the city know that he still had the thunder and lightning with him, as soon as it became dark ordered a general discharge of his artillery. " The thunders of the ordnance, reverberating among the buildings, and shaking them to their foundations, the stench of the sulphurous vapor that rolled in volumes above the walls of the court-yard, reminded the inhabitants of the explosions of the great volcanoes, and filled the hearts of the Aztecs with dismay. It told them that they had, in the bosom of their city, those dread beings whose path had been marked with desolation, who could call down the thunderbolts to consume their enemies."

Cortes did it undoubtedly for the express purpose of impressing the natives, at the outset, with awe of the supernatural powers of the Spaniards.

The next day Cortes returned the visit of the Emperor. He found the Emperor's palace an extensive group of stone buildings not exceeding one story in height. It was so spacious (says one who was with Cortes), that although he visited it more than once for the express purpose, he had been too much fatigued each time by wandering through the apartments ever to see the whole of it. It was built of stone put together with cement, and was ornamented with marble, and on the façade over the principal entrance were sculptured the arms of Montezuma, an eagle bearing an ocelot in his talons.

In the courts many fountains of crystal water were playing, and they supplied more than a hundred baths in the interior of the palace. Crowds of Aztec nobles were sauntering about in these squares and outer halls, in their attendance upon the court. The apartments were of immense size, though not lofty. The ceilings were of various sorts of odorous woods ingeniously carved, and the floors were covered with mats made of the palm leaf. Some of the walls were hung with richly colored tapestry, some with the skins of wild animals, and others with gorgeous draperies of featherwork wrought in imitation of birds, insects, and flowers, that would compare favorably with the tapestries of Flanders. Spices and incense made the air fragrant.

The visitors were obliged to cover their gay attire

with a coarse cloak and to remove their shoes before being presented. Advancing in this condition, and with downcast eyes, they approached the Emperor, whom they found at the farther end of a spacious apartment, the walls of which were hung with beautiful tapestries, and the wooden ceiling exquisitely carved.

Cortes made a long speech to the Emperor upon the duties of his religion, but it had little or no effect upon Montezuma, for he was wedded to his own, having been a priest when he was elected emperor. He listened with silent attention until Cortes had finished, and then replied in the following language:

"I know you have talked like this wherever you have been. I doubt not that your God is a good being. My gods are also good. What you say about the creation of the world, is the same as I have been taught to believe. It is not worth while to further discuss the matter. My ancestors were not the original proprietors of this land. They have occupied it but a few ages. They were led here by a great being, who, after giving them laws, and ruling over the nation for a time, withdrew to the regions where the sun rises. He declared on his departure, that he, or his descendants, would again visit this country and resume his empire. Your wonderful deeds, your fair complexion, and the quarter from whence you come, all show that you are his descendants. If I have resisted your visit to the capital, it was because I heard such accounts of your cruelties; that you sent the lightning to consume my people, or crushed them to death under the feet of ferocious animals. I am now convinced that these were idle tales, and that you are kind and generous in your natures; that you are mortals, but of a different race, wiser and more valiant, and for this I honor you."

Then smiling, he added : " You, too, have been told, perhaps, that I am a god, and dwell in palaces of gold and silver. But you see it is false. My houses, though large, are of stone and wood like those of others, and as to my body, you see it is flesh and bone like yours. It is true, I have a great empire, inherited from my ancestors, lands, and gold, and silver. But your sovereign beyond the waters is, I know, the rightful lord of all. I rule in his name. You are his ambassador. You and your brethren shall share these things with me. Rest now from your labors. You are here in your own dwellings, and everything shall be provided for your subsistence. I will see that your wishes shall be obeyed in the same way as my own."

On finishing his speech, the once proud and haughty monarch's eyes were filled with tears.

Before dismissing his visitors, Montezuma, as usual, made them handsome presents, amounting, says Bernald Diaz (who was one of the party) to at least two heavy collars of the precious metal for the share of the poorest soldier.

Diaz also says : " We were all touched by the emotion displayed by Montezuma, as well as by his princely spirit of liberality, and on the way to our

quarters could talk of nothing but the gentle breed-
ing and courtesy of the Indian monarch."

"In the appearance of the capital, its massive, yet
elegant architecture, its luxurious social accommodations, and its activity in trade, Cortes saw and
recognized the proofs of the intellectual progress,
mechanical skill, and enlarged resources of an old
and opulent community."

There was a square set apart for a market, large
enough to accommodate forty thousand people.
There, on market-days, could be found persons from
every part of the empire, with their wares for sale or
exchange. The goldsmiths and jewellers, the potters,
the painters, the stone-cutters, the hunters, the
fishermen, the fruiterers, the mat- and chair-makers,
and the florists,—each with a separate place assigned
them. The workmanship of the artists in gold and
silver, also those in embroidery, tapestry, curtains,
coverlets, etc., equalled, if it did not surpass, that
of Europe.

Their money was a piece of metal resembling tin,
stamped or made into the shape of the Roman letter
T, and quills filled with gold dust.

There was also in the city a menagerie, owned by
the government, in which were to be seen specimens
of all the wild beasts and birds of the country.
This collection was so large that it required the services of five hundred men daily to take care for it.

Aqueducts brought water into the city for the use
of the entire populace. The number of inhabitants
in the city was variously estimated at from two to

three hundred thousand. The dishes used by the common people were made of clay, and those of the Emperor were of gold and silver. The women were dressed in loose garments reaching from the neck to the feet, and held at the waist·by a girdle. The skirt was sometimes bordered with beautiful fringes. A light flowing drapery was occasionally worn over this, reaching from the shoulders to the ankles in front, and trailing upon the ground behind, a dress that would be becoming in any civilized land.

17

CHAPTER XVIII.

IT will be remembered that Cortes promised at one time to repay Montezuma for his munificent presents in " good works." His indebtedness was large, for while in the City of Mexico he divided the spoils among his officers and men, and upon appraising them for such division they were found to amount to one hundred and sixty-two thousand " pesos de oro," independent of the fine ornaments and jewelry, the value of which Cortes computes at five hundred thousand ducats more. There were also five hundred marks of silver, in plate, drinking cups, and other articles of luxury.

The whole amount reduced to the currency of the United States, and making allowance for the difference in the value of gold since the beginning of the sixteenth century, was about six million, three hundred thousand dollars, or in English currency, one million, four hundred and seventeen thousand pounds sterling.

Cortes repaid this debt, besides the one of gratitude he owed to Montezuma for his kind reception and care upon reaching the capital, by arresting the Emperor, and making him a prisoner in his camp, upon the slight pretence that he had connived at the act of a cazique upon the coast in the murder of two of the Spanish soldiers left at the little fort at Villa Rica.

After making the Emperor a prisoner, he obliged him to order the arrest of this cazique, and have him brought to the capital. When the cazique arrived, the Emperor was compelled to turn the cazique, his son, and fifteen chiefs who accompanied him, over to Cortes to be dealt with by him; and this " Christian soldier " condemned them all to be burned alive in the area before the palace, which was done. This was an act of cruelty worse than any ever committed by Indians, because it was done by men claiming to be civilized.

So unjustifiably barbarous was this act, that it nearly annihilated the belief in the minds of many of the natives that the Spaniards were the descendants of the good " God of the Air," and would have resulted in an immediate uprising, had not Montezuma, by the command of Cortes, issued orders which quieted the populace.

But another wanton and cruel butchery soon brought on the crisis. Cortes left the city for a visit to the coast. He placed one of his officers, Alvarado, in command during his absence. While Alvarado was in command, the Aztecs desired to hold a customary annual festival in the court-yard of the great temple. As the city was then under command of the Spaniards, they asked permission of Alvarado, which was granted on condition that they should bear no arms, and have no sacrifices.

On the appointed day, the Aztecs assembled to the number of about six hundred (some writers say a thousand). The company was composed almost entirely of the rich and the officials of the city, attired in their gala dress and wearing gold necklaces, armlets, anklets, and precious stones in profusion.

Alvarado and his Spanish soldiers, fully armed, attended as spectators; some remained outside the walls, some at the gates as if by chance, and others mingled with the crowd. The fact of the Spaniards being armed excited no suspicion, as they always carried their arms when about the city. When the Aztecs became fully engrossed in the dances, at a given signal Alvarado and his men rushed upon them, slaughtering their unarmed victims without the slightest pity or mercy. Those who ran to the gates were hewn down by the soldiers stationed there, while those who climbed the wall were shot by the soldiers stationed on the outside for that purpose. "The pavement," says a writer who witnessed it, "ran with streams of blood, like water in a heavy shower." Not an Aztec of all that gay company was left alive, and after the slaughter the civilized and Christianized Spaniards rifled the dead of their valuable ornaments.

This most inhuman and atrocious act opened the eyes of the deluded Aztecs living in the City of Mexico, to the fact that the Spaniards were most assuredly *not* the descendants of the good "God of the Air," and from that moment the old tradition began to lose its hold upon their minds. The Emperor

Montezuma having died while a prisoner, the citizens, on the night of July 1, 1520, rose in their might and drove the Spanish invaders out of their city with fearful slaughter. The attack occurred after Cortes had returned to the city, and that any of the Spaniards escaped with their lives is undoubtedly due to his generalship.

Cortes had been reinforced by the soldiers, horses, and cannon of Narvaez, so that he had at that time about one thousand foot-soldiers and one hundred horses, and ten large and small cannon.

Of this force, he lost on the night he was driven from the city, four hundred and fifty Spaniards, all but twenty of his horses, and all his cannon.

I think this event proves conclusively that had it not been for the supineness of the Emperor, caziques, and people, caused by the tradition, or prophecy, in regard to the good "God of the Air," and their belief that the Spaniards were his descendants, Cortes could never have advanced far into the country of the Aztecs.

It was this belief, which still lingered in the minds of the caziques, chiefs, and people of the country, that enabled Cortes to raise another army after his expulsion from the capital, and finally to conquer Guatemozin, the chief who had assumed full command after the death of Montezuma.

Cortes promised this chief personal protection, if he would capitulate and cease fighting, but in place of such protection, he delivered Guatemozin to his men to be tortured, in the hope of compelling him

to tell where the supposed vast wealth of the city
had been buried,—he from the first protesting that
he did not know, except that one large dial of gold
had been thrown into the garden-pond at his palace.
They burned his feet with slow fire, and tortured
him most unmercifully but he told of nothing more,
for the reason, as he said, that he did not know the
whereabouts of any other treasure.

Cortes subsequently gave another evidence of his
manner of keeping sacred promises, by hanging the
chief, with several of his nobles, to a tree by the
roadside.

The fall of the City of Mexico, which Cortes accomplished with the aid of the natives who yet
believed in the legend, practically ended the existence of the Aztecs.

The Spaniards having conquered and obtained
possession, began flocking into the country, and
established a government not a step in advance of
the one they had destroyed ; and in regard to the
sacrifice of human life, revolting as it is, it is
quite questionable whether a greater number of
victims can be charged to the Aztecs, or the Spaniards, when we take into the account all who were
put to death in Spain, in the Netherlands, and in
every other country in which the Spaniards ever had
power or influence ; and in the manner of the killing the Aztecs were far in advance of the Spaniards
in the scale of humanity. They executed their victims in the quickest possible manner, with the body
placed in the most convenient position for doing it

speedily and with the least suffering; while the Spaniards caused their victims to suffer the untold tortures of the rack, slow fire, and numberless other most exquisite, ingenious, and excruciating modes of torture. The method that would keep the poor victim alive the longest, under the most severe suffering, was always the favorite with them. Both sacrificed their victims in the name of religion, as an act pleasing to the deities they worshipped, but the Spaniards were far more fiendish and cruel than the Indians, although they called themselves civilized.

The Aztecs were completely crushed, so that the few who remain to-day are mere nomads in the country that was once their own, and the seat of the most extensive agriculture and remarkable horticulture then known to the world.

The evidences of their civilization have nearly all been scattered to the winds. Even their histories and writings, with few exceptions, were gathered in piles on the plazas in the different cities and burned by the so-called civilized and enlightened Spaniards.

But from the few records that escaped destruction, and from the other signs of civilization, as exhibited in the accounts we have of their government, architecture, horticulture, religious belief, and system of education, I am firmly of the opinion that, had America never been discovered by Europeans, the civilization existing in Mexico would in time have grown to the same perfection it has now attained in Europe and America, and spread until it had brought every nation, tribe, and people of this continent within its healthful and enlightened influence.

There can be no doubt that our own ancestors were once as ignorant and wild as any of the tribes of North America, and that they passed through the various stages of semi-civilization we have seen existing here ; yet, in the course of time, they emerged from that barbarism and mental darkness into the light and civilization of the present day. They had no help or light from others ; it was all accomplished through the workings of their own brain ; and no one will dispute the fact that the Indians of North America have exhibited as strong and powerful intellects as any human beings ever possessed prior to education and culture.

In the United States and Canada, the respective governments have to some extent tried to ameliorate the forlorn condition of the Indians within their borders.

The government of the United States adopted the plan of dealing with them as " dependent nations," making treaties with them as with a foreign power. Owing to the weakness of the " dependent nations," and their not being able to enforce their "treaty rights," this system has proved a grand farce.

The government has violated the provisions of these "solemn treaties" whenever it suited its convenience to do so.

When the Indians were placed upon reservations, where it was impossible for them to obtain food and clothing for themselves, the government, in payment for the land ceded to it by the Indians, "solemnly" provided in the treaties to furnish them with these necessaries.

It must be remembered that one of the sacred promises in every treaty has been that white men should be kept from settling or trespassing upon the reservations, and that the Indians should be protected from the white man's avarice, fraud, and assaults.

How well the government has kept these promises the Indian wars during the past few years attest. The great majority, if not all of them, have arisen from the white man's trespasses, or from the fact that the Indians were starving upon the reservations, and in many of their appeals to the government they have said that they had rather die upon the war-path than by the slow, lingering tortures of starvation.

It is a well-known fact that when an Indian has plenty to eat he is a quiet individual, and, from my personal acquaintance with them, I think I may safely assert that there would not have been any wars had the government faithfully kept its promises in these two particulars alone.

I am corroborated in this statement by Professor Seelye, formerly United States Commissioner of Indian Affairs, who said: "There has not been a war in fifty years in which the whites have not been the aggressors."

The other grievances could have been settled by giving time for arbitration, but an empty stomach brooks no delay. It cannot wait for the slow process of negotiation,

The dealing with them as "nations," instead of as citizens, for many years past, has been the source of much misunderstanding. It is true, they could not have been admitted at once to full citizenship, but they might have enjoyed a restricted citizenship.

Canada has dealt with the Indians within her borders as "subjects of the crown" for many years. They are under the power and control of her laws, and entitled to the rights and privileges of "subjects," with a few restrictions suited to their condition. The result has been that she has had scarcely any trouble with them. She has also been careful in making promises, making fewer than the United States, but strictly keeping such as she did make.

The Indians charge all the frauds and outrages committed upon them by the agents, contractors, inspectors, and trespassers, to the government, for they do not understand why a government cannot control those in its employ.

It is useless to discuss the question as to whether the Indians could have been, twenty-five years ago, made citizens, with some restrictions, but there can be no question that it could have been done as soon as they had been placed upon reservations.

As now situated upon the reservations, they are practically without law. Their chiefs are almost powerless, and there is no government to take their place. An attempt has been made at some of the agencies to establish Indian courts, and the effort has met with some success. It is a step in the right direction. In my judgment, a better method than the one now being tried would be to have a regularly appointed district judge who should hold court at every agency within his district at least once in six months, with an Indian judge as associate, such Indian judge to be appointed for each agency. All juries passing upon matters between white men and Indians should be composed of an equal number of white men and Indians. The Indian judge should be empowered to hear and try all petty matters between the Indians, and have an Indian jury. The agent should be empowered to carry out the decisions of the court. This plan, it seems to me, would insure justice, and teach the Indians our laws and the manner of their enforcement, thus gradually accustoming them to our laws and our mode of administering justice.

Everything done with regard to the Indians should be with the ulterior motive of making them citizens at the earliest possible moment.

The government is also trying to induce the Indians to become farmers. This is also a step in the right direction, but it is foiled to a great extent by the present manner of teaching them. An act of Congress provides that assistant farmers shall be sent among the Indians to teach them farming. How this has been done is well illustrated by what was told me within the past year by a Senator of the United States, who was one of a committee appointed to investigate this subject. He said they found one of these teachers who, when asked how to plant turnips, said: "Cut them into small pieces and put a few of the pieces in a hill." How long would it take Indians to become self-supporting farmers under such instruction? The difficulty is that such appointments are frequently made for political reasons, and with entire disregard to any fitness of the appointee for the work.

The law provides for the inspection of supplies; but, from some hidden cause, the goods that are served to the Indians fall far short of the quality paid for by the government. It is not so with supplies furnished the army.

The government of the United States has established and maintains two hundred and forty-six schools for the Indians, and there are several other schools that take Indian children under contract with the Indian Bureau, and, during the year 1890, the government appropriated one million three hundred and sixty-four thousand dollars for the education of Indian children, and in 1892 increased the sum to two million two hundred and sixteen thousand dollars.

But it is not my purpose to give statistics, I mention the above merely to show what is being done within the United States and its territories for the education of the Indians.

Neither do I intend to charge *all* Indian agents with dishonesty or unfaithfulness. There *may* be some honest and honorable ones (naturalists tell us there are white crows), but when the fact is patent —established beyond dispute—that the Indians are *everywhere* cheated and swindled, we cannot but suspect the persons who would naturally profit pecuniarily by such swindling. It is natural to look for the motive governing men's actions; and what honest motive could induce a man to banish himself and family from all the blessings, privileges, and enjoyments of civilization, for the mere pittance of fifteen hundred dollars a year, when most, if not all of which would have to be expended in living, is beyond my ken; unless, indeed, he goes partly as a missionary, expecting to receive the balance of his earnings when he reaches the " Happy Hunting-Grounds."

I have been among Indians while they were yet in their primitive state, and can fully corroborate the reports made concerning them by those who first visited this continent, that *in* their primitive state they are a good-natured, quiet people, well disposed towards white men, and in my opinion, had they been fairly dealt with, they would never have given the whites any trouble or annoyance.

I also believe that had the treatment inaugurated by Governor Penn been universally adopted from the first, the Indians, as fast as civilization reached them, would have mingled with us and become a part of the body politic, like the Negro, only upon a higher plane, for no such race prejudice ever existed against them as has always existed against the Negro. There was nothing to prevent their becoming a part of our people, except the bitter hatred engendered in their bosoms by the unjust and cruel treatment they received at the hands of the whites; a hatred that would, if possible, last beyond the grave, as was said by the old Indian chief of whom I have before spoken.

They would have made good and useful citizens, instead of being what they are now—isolated communities having little governments of their own, or shut up on reservations in a semi-civilized condition, and under charge of the government as wards.

They have shown themselves capable of civilized self-government, as witness the Aztecs in Mexico in early times, and the Senecas in the State of New York, the Cherokees, Choctaws, Chickasaws, and others that might be mentioned, of the present day.

As to those who have not yet entered upon a civilized life, there is no question that, with but few exceptions, their minds are filled with animosity against us ; and as we cannot justly blame them for this, and as it is impossible to redeem the past, we must deal with them as they now are, having due regard to their future as well as their present good. Our judgment in determining what is for their good is much better than their own, and they must submit to it.

Those who are opposed to having their children attend school or receive instruction in mechanical or agricultural pursuits, must be compelled to submit to our better judgment in the matter.

I cannot too strongly reiterate my belief that it would be for the best interest of the Indians, no less than for the government, to make them citizens as soon as possible, amenable to, and protected by the same laws as the white citizen, with perhaps some few exceptions, particularly in regard to the alienation of land.

I am heartily in favor of giving the War Department of the government full and *entire* control of the Indians, for several reasons :

First—The officers of the army are appointed for life, conditioned upon good behavior; and this relieves them from the temptation of trying to become rich in haste, lest they be removed from office on the incoming of a new administration.

Second—These officers would have every incentive to conduct matters in such a manner as to avoid hostilities. The army suffers great trials and hardships in case of an Indian war, and there is no glory to be won in fighting Indians. The great majority of army officers, and I think I may say *all* who have had any experience with Indians, are of the same opinion as Major-General Wool (from whose report I have quoted)—"that if the Indians were fairly and justly dealt with, we would have no trouble with them."

Third—There would be no more Indian agents whose only qualifications for the place consist in being good political wire-pullers.

Fourth—All provisions and supplies for the Indians would pass through the same inspection as supplies for the army, and there would then be none of the present inspectors who, for reasons known to themselves (and surmised by others), allow the contractors to purchase poor, old, and worthless cattle at from three to five dollars per head (about what their hides are worth), and furnish them to the Indians under a contract with the government which called for good fat cattle, and at a price adequate for that class.

It would also put a stop to the furnishing of inferior blankets, and to the notorious inferiority in all other supplies for which the government pays prices that should secure good articles.

Fifth—It would be much less expensive to the government. The army is paid whether active or idle, and the employment of some of its officers as bureau officials and Indian agents, and some of its non-commissioned officers and men as assistants, would save much of the money now paid to others doing that work, and it would be more economically performed in every way, even though the army list should be increased to furnish the necessary number of officers.

I am also in favor of establishing practical agricultural schools at many, if not all of the Indian agencies, and compelling all the Indians between certain ages to attend them a sufficient length of time to learn how to cultivate a farm successfully. The more schools established, the sooner the desired result would be attained.

I am opposed to the allotment of land in severalty, except to those Indians who are sufficiently educated in the art of farming to till their allotment reasonably well, and who would be able to make a living from it for themselves and family.

Putting an Indian upon a piece of land with the

necessary implements, before he knows enough about farming to till the land properly, and then telling him to go to work and make a living for himself and family, or starve, would be like putting the proper materials and tools into the hands of one of us who does not understand electricity, and telling him to make a dynamo, or starve—I think most of us would be likely to starve. Yet the latter proposition is as reasonable as the former.

The argument against agricultural schools would be the expense. It would be tedious to give a list of figures to show that this argument should have little weight. Suffice it to say, that the money the government now has in its treasury belonging to the Indians, the amount of which is one hundred and thirteen million dollars, with that which would be received from the sale of the surplus lands after the allotments were made, would be amply sufficient to cover all the expenses.

It may be said we have no right to use the money belonging to the Indians.

In answer to this permit me to say that I deem it not only the right, but the positive duty of the government to use the money belonging to Indians in such a way as will accomplish their greatest good; and how can it be used to give to them and their posterity a greater or more lasting benefit than in teaching them practical mechanics, and how to properly till the soil, thus preparing them to be self-supporting citizens in the not far-distant future.

It has been my endeavor in these pages to refresh the memories of my readers in regard to a few of the many wrongs which the Indians have suffered at the hands of the white men, and to bring them to view these things from *their* standpoint, looking at events through *their eyes ;* hoping thus to lessen the blame attached to them for their acts of retaliation. And I have had in mind the further purpose of so enlisting your sympathies, that all the influence you each possess may be used to urge upon the government the necessity of changing the present management of the Indians, and of adding to the number of manual-training schools for them, and to hasten also the establishment of practical agricultural schools at many (if not all) of the Indian agencies in the land,—as the surest, cheapest, quickest, most humane, and most practical way of solving the Indian problem.

We are a great and powerful people—mighty among the nations of the earth. On account of one great national sin we have passed through an ordeal of chastisement and suffering which cost us rivers of blood, and millions of treasure—an ordeal from which one section of our country has not even yet, after the lapse of more than a quarter of a century, entirely recovered. Let us no longer rest under the shadow of another national sin, against another unfortunate race.

The Red-men are fast passing away. The beautiful land of their nativity will soon know them no more. It is beyond our power to undo the wrongs inflicted upon them by our ancestors ; but we can, and ought to be just—even generous—towards the few who are still with us. Let us hasten to remove from our national escutcheon its one foul blot —the stigma of inhumanity and injustice towards the proud but hapless Indian.

THE END.